SHARED PEDAGOGICAL RESPONSIBILITY

SHARED PEDAGOGICAL RESPONSIBILITY

Edited by

Hans van Crombrugge
Wouter Vandenhole
Jan C.M. Willems

Other contributors

Ineke Boerefijn
Martine F. Delfos
Doret de Ruyter

Antwerp – Oxford – Portland

Distribution for the UK:
Hart Publishing Ltd.
16C Worcester Place
Oxford OX1 2JW
UK
Tel.: +44 1865 51 75 30
Fax: +44 1865 51 07 10

Distribution for Switzerland and Germany:
Schulthess Verlag
Zwingliplatz 2
CH-8022 Zürich
Switzerland
Tel.: +41 1 251 93 36
Fax: +41 1 261 63 94

Distribution for the USA and Canada:
International Specialized Book Services
920 NE 58th Ave Suite 300
Portland, OR 97213
USA
Tel.: +1 800 944 6190 (toll free)
Tel.: +1 503 287 3093
Fax: +1 503 280 8832
Email: info@isbs.com

Distribution for other countries:
Intersentia Publishers
Groenstraat 31
BE-2640 Mortsel
Belgium
Tel.: +32 3 680 15 50
Fax: +32 3 658 71 21

Shared Pedagogical Responsibility
Hans van Crombrugge, Wouter Vandenhole and Jan C.M. Willems (eds.)

© 2008 Intersentia
   Antwerp – Oxford – Portland
   www.intersentia.com

Cover photograph © iStockphoto.com/Mehmet Ali Cida – "Relay Race"

ISBN 978-90-5095-813-4
D/2008/7849/66
NUR 820

No part of this book may be reproduced in any form, by print, photoprint, microfilm or any other means, without written permission from the publisher.

TABLE OF CONTENTS

INTRODUCTION
     Hans van Crombrugge, Wouter Vandenhole, Jan C.M. Willems 1

THE UPBRINGING PLEDGE AS A FRAMEWORK FOR THE PARENT-CHILD RELATIONSHIP
     Hans van Crombrugge 5

1. Introduction... 5
2. Upbringing Pledge and the Rights of the Child: Some Propositions 7
   2.1. The Pedagogical Responsibility of the State 7
   2.2. Parenthood... 8
   2.3. Supporting the Parents................................... 9
   2.4. Concrete Proposals..................................... 10
3. Discussion 11

WHAT MAY PARENTS BE ASKED TO PLEDGE?
The Convention on the Rights of the Child as a Source of Parental Duties and Responsibilities
     Jan C.M. Willems 17

1. Introduction.. 17
   1.1. Transism... 18
   1.2. A List of Responsibilities 20
2. State Empowerment and Responsibilization Obligations 21
   2.1. State Obligations...................................... 22
   2.2. Trias Pedagogica 23
   2.3. Empowerment Obligations 24
3. Fifty-Plus-One Parental Duties and Responsibilities 25
4. Conclusion 32
Appendix 1. Eight Essential Parental Responsibilities..................... 33
Appendix 2. Ten Parental Responsibilities & Ten Parental Rights 35

CHILDREN'S RIGHTS, PARENTAL RESPONSIBILITIES AND STATE OBLIGATIONS: A COUNCIL OF EUROPE PERSPECTIVE
Wouter Vandenhole 37

1. Human Rights of Children 39
2. Human Rights of Parents... 43
3. Responsibilities of Parents... 47
4. Obligations of the State 48
   4.1. Obligation to Protect Against Corporal Punishment............. 48
   4.2. Obligation to Protect Children Against Neglect and Abuse 50
   4.3. Obligation to Respect Family Life 51
   4.4. Obligation to Assist in Enforcement of Access Arrangements 52
   4.5. Obligations Relating to Particularly Vulnerable Groups of Children 52
   4.6. Obligations Relating to Equality.............................. 53
   4.7. Obligations Related to Protection of the Family 53
5. Social Cohesion Framework 54
6. Conclusion: An Upbringing Pledge: Optional, Recommended or Mandatory? 55

RECONCILING HUMAN RIGHTS OF WOMEN AND CHILDREN
Ineke Boerefijn... 57

1. Introduction... 57
2. Equality of the Sexes.. 58
3. The Position of Women in the Public Sphere 61
   3.1. Employment and Economic Independence of Women............ 61
   3.2. Participation in Public and Political Life 62
   3.3. Education 63
   3.4. The Upbringing Pledge and Equality of Women and Men in the Public Sphere 64
4. The Position of Women in the Family.............................. 65
   4.1. Introduction.. 65
   4.2. Equal Right to Enter Into Marriage, Equal Rights During Marriage and at Its Dissolution 66
   4.3. Sexual and Reproductive Rights............................... 68
   4.4. Violence Against Women 70
   4.5. An Upbringing Pledge and Women's Right to Equality in the Family... 71
5. Towards a Human Rights Approach 72

FROM PARENT TO GROUP PARENT
Parenthood (and Upbringing Pledge) in the Virtual Environment
  Martine F. Delfos 75

1. From Parent to Group Parent 75
2. The Virtual Environment 77
3. Educational Authority 79
4. The Need to Form Attachments 80
5. Virtual Life Enschede 82
6. Conclusion 84

References 84

THE UPBRINGING PLEDGE AND THE FLOURISHING OF CHILDREN AND PARENTS
  Doret de Ruyter 87

1. Introduction 87
2. The Concept of 'Upbringing Pledge' 88
  2.1. The Person Making the Promise: The Promiser 89
  2.2. The Promisee 92
  2.3. The Content of a Promise 94
3. Promises and Duties 94
4. The Upbringing Pledge and Quality of Upbringing 96
5. The Upbringing Pledge in a Liberal Democracy 98
6. Conclusion 101

Bibliography 102

THE UPBRINGING PLEDGE: A RITUAL IN SUPPORT OF PARENTS
A Rejoinder to Doret de Ruyter's Critical Analysis
  Hans van Crombrugge 105

1. Introduction 105
2. The Upbringing Pledge as Ritual: The Institution of Parenthood 106
3. The Upbringing Pledge and Its Assumptions: Obligations Versus Facts . 108
4. The Upbringing Pledge and Its Stakeholders: Everyone is Committed Together 111
5. The Pledge and Its Binding Character: The Demand of the Child as a Moral Claim 112

6. The Pledge Improves the Quality of Upbringing: It Confirms and Establishes Respect for the Rights of the Child 114
7. The Upbringing Pledge in a Liberal Democracy: The Upbringing Obligation Imposed by the Government........................... 116

INTRODUCTION

Hans van Crombrugge, Wouter Vandenhole, Jan C.M. Willems

Human rights tend to focus on the relationship between individual and state: the individual is the rights-holder, while the state is the duty-holder. Children's rights bring a third player much more into the picture, namely parents. Although legally speaking they are not duty-holders under the UN Convention on the Rights of the Child (CRC), they do have a number of responsibilities under the CRC and other human rights instruments. States may have obligations to turn these parental responsibilities into national legal duties if that is needed to improve the legal and social position of children.

Child rearing may still be considered by many to be within the private domain, i.e. a matter of concern only within the relationship between children and their parents, with the exception of instances of child abuse or neglect.

In this volume, child rearing responsibilities are examined in the light of children's rights and (other) human rights. All contributions focus in particular on the proposal made in 2004 by Van Crombrugge to introduce an upbringing (or parenting) pledge.[1] Two conferences were dedicated to this proposal and its social and legal (human rights) context: the first in 2006[2] and the second in 2007.[3] This book builds on the papers presented at the 2007 conference.

---

[1] Van Crombrugge, H. (2004), "Ik zal er zijn voor jou"; Van huwelijksgezin naar contractueel gezin, *Rondom Gezin*, 25, pp. 32–50. An overview of the genesis of the proposal of the upbringing pledge may be found in: Van Crombrugge, H. (2007), Van huwelijksgezin naar opvoedingsbelofte, Over de institutionalisering van ouders als opvoeders, in: Colpin, H. & Van Crombrugge, H. (Eds.), *Gezinnen en gezinspedagogiek – Geboeid door verscheidenheid, Liber amicorum prof. dr. Lieve Vandemeulebroecke* (pp. 19–41), Antwerpen-Apeldoorn: Garant.

[2] Jennes, G. & Hertecant, B. (Eds.) (2006), *Van huwelijkscontract naar opvoedingsbelofte*, Brussel: Hoger Instituut voor Gezinswetenschappen/Vlaams Centrum voor het Welzijn van Kinderen en Gezinnen.

[3] Van Crombrugge, H., Vandenhole, W. & Willems, J. (Eds.), (2007), *Gedeelde pedagogische verantwoordelijkheid; De opvoedingsbelofte in het licht van de rechten van de mens en de rechten van het kind*, Brussel: Hoger Instituut voor Gezinswetenschappen/Universiteit Antwerpen/Universiteit Maastricht.

Hans van Crombrugge, Wouter Vandenhole, Jan C.M. Willems

The proposal for a mandatory upbringing pledge is outlined and explained in the first chapter of this book. Van Crombrugge's starting point is that child rearing can no longer be seen as exclusively and automatically linked to biological parenthood in the context of the civil marriage family. He sees the upbringing pledge as a social institution and legal framework through which the commitment of parents and their responsibility to care for and raise their children can be expressed. It would allow future parents to explicitly and publicly commit themselves to parenthood as facilitated, supported and legislated by the state on the basis of the rights of the child. The upbringing pledge contains not only a statement of lasting commitment towards their children, but also an explicit declaration of commitment to respect and promote the rights of the child both as a person and as a human being who is utterly dependent upon his or her parents for his or her well-being and the development of his or her personality. By means of the upbringing pledge as a child rights-based social institution, the responsibilities of society and the state towards both parents and children are re-affirmed as well.

In a first move, the attribution and, especially, distribution of child rearing (or pedagogical) responsibility is scrutinized in the light of children's rights and human rights law by Willems, Vandenhole and Boerefijn. Willems sheds light on the distribution of pedagogical responsibility from the perspective of the UN Convention on the Rights of the Child in particular. He considers the upbringing pledge as an example of a child rights-based approach to parenting. Such an approach combines two elements: empowerment of (future) parents, and their so-called responsibilization. In Willems's view, the upbringing pledge fits the overall child rights' agenda of fighting transism. "Transism, or transgenerational discrimination, refers to a state not adequately addressing socio-economic and, more specifically, socio-emotional differences between (young) parents." He then distills fifty-one parental responsibilities from the CRC's principles and provisions, so as to clarify the actual and potential content of an upbringing pledge. As to the upbringing pledge, and its emancipatory potential in particular, Willems clearly is a believer.

Vandenhole examines, from a Council of Europe perspective, the interplay of children's rights and human rights with a special focus on the upbringing of children. He analyzes consecutively the human rights of children, the human rights and responsibilities of parents/caregivers, and the obligations of the state, in an attempt to arrive at a clearer framework of the distribution of child rearing responsibilities between, in particular, the parents or caregivers, and the state. He concludes that the human rights instruments of the Council of Europe and the way they have been interpreted by their respective monitoring mechanisms do not reject nor lend explicit support to the idea of an upbringing pledge.

Boerefijn zooms in on a long-standing, real or perceived, tension between children's rights and women's rights. She advocates for a more constructive approach to the CRC and CEDAW (the UN Women's Convention), in which both instruments are seen as reconcilable and even mutually reinforcing. This means that the CRC should not be seen as an instrument that stereotypes women as mothers (to which, by the way, the CRC testifies in explicit terms), nor that the CEDAW should be perceived as an instrument that subordinates the interests of children to the rights of women (as is evidenced by CEDAW itself). She therefore submits, without further substantiating her claim, that advancing the position of women positively influences the position of children. An upbringing pledge is only acceptable from a women's rights perspective to the extent that it is "part of an all-encompassing policy aimed at improving the position of women in society and the family" and takes the unequal position of women and men in society and in the family sufficiently into account.

After this legal analysis from a plurality of human rights perspectives, Delfos pleads for opening up the discussion, not only by bringing in the perspective of other disciplines, but mainly by moving beyond the family and the state as actors in child rearing. She points out in particular the massive impact on child rearing of the virtual environment. She therefore forwards the idea of a much broader upbringing pledge: a commitment of adults to develop standards and values for the virtual environment, so that children are protected against harmful information and material.

De Ruyter in her self-labelled critical analysis by an analytical philosopher of child rearing, immediately focuses on the upbringing pledge. She starts off by admitting that "it is good practice to demarcate a significant change in the life of persons with a ritual," which in the case of novel parenthood would then be an upbringing (parenting) pledge. She then raises two crucial questions: whether an upbringing pledge is able to make a positive contribution to the quality of child rearing and whether a mandatory upbringing pledge can be justified in a liberal democratic state. On both accounts she answers in the negative. It is, thus, left to the reader to conclude, on the basis of the preceding contributions, whether a human rights and especially child rights perspective would lead to a more positive outcome.

The final word is to the intellectual father and main promoter of the upbringing pledge, Van Crombrugge. He responds in particular to De Ruyter's analytical criticism. In his second contribution, the upbringing pledge is elaborated as a ritual. From this perspective, the meaningfulness of a mandatory upbringing pledge is developed as an instrument for improving the quality of child rearing.

In his reply, it appears that the disagreement with De Ruyter has not only to do with different views on the role of the state toward families (i.e. traditional rather than child rights based), but also with different views on the concepts of child rearing and the quality of child rearing. Van Crombrugge defines the quality of upbringing in terms of the characteristics of the interaction; to De Ruyter upbringing is an instrumental relation of which the quality is defined in terms of the instrumental value of the interaction for the flourishing of the child.

The contributions to this book show that there is no easy answer to the question whether, and if so under which conditions, we should be in favour of an upbringing pledge. Some interesting questions and tensions have been identified, and a (sometimes only preliminary) attempt has been undertaken to address them. One such question is whether the Convention on the Rights of the Child imposes a normative model of upbringing on the government of a state party. Van Crombrugge rejects this idea, while Willems seems to see some value in it, that is, insofar that it is built on multidisciplinary knowledge (e.g. of developmental psychology and psychopathology, best practices of parenting support, mental health care, and so forth). Another question is how women's rights and children's rights relate to each other, for there is persistent fear that children's rights may come at the expense of women's rights. Here, too, the key to address this fear is most likely to be found in a multidisciplinary approach rather than within the narrow precepts of a single discipline. Since a conflict of rights of two groups which are often considered to be vulnerable, and therefore in need of protection and tailor-made rights, is always possible, it automatically pops up whenever new ideas, such as an upbringing pledge, are explored. Also the question of the just and balanced distribution of pedagogical responsibility between the state and parents will not be easy to answer in the time to come – if it ever will be. Since children's rights, especially in relation to responsible parenthood, are far from crystallized, they may offer no more than the direction in which answers may be found – although the importance of this should not be underestimated. So, the debate will – and should – go on. This is certainly to be hoped as far as the proposal of the upbringing pledge is concerned, which may well serve as a focus and a catalyst for this much needed debate.

Antwerp – Brussels – Maastricht
May 2008

THE UPBRINGING PLEDGE AS A FRAMEWORK FOR THE PARENT-CHILD RELATIONSHIP

Hans van Crombrugge[*]

1. INTRODUCTION

In order to develop, children are entrusted to people who care for and guide them. Parents or guardians cannot be easily interchanged. Permanence is an essential quality of the bond between the child and his or her first parents or guardians. If the lasting commitment of parents for the well-being and growth of children is so important, the government must do everything it can to strengthen the development, preservation and quality of this parent-child bond. There are many instruments that policy makers have available to organize this support. A unique – and in our opinion underestimated – means that the government has at its disposal is the creation of an institutional framework in which the parental commitment and pedagogical responsibility for the child can be expressed.

The traditional framework for this was marriage. The civil marriage family was a societal institution that regulated not only the life together of two adults. It also had a clear-cut pedagogical objective and legitimacy: ensuring that the children that resulted from the relationship were cared for and brought up properly. The civil marriage family created rights and obligations for the partners as well as for the government. In this way, the civil marriage family was an instrument for general pedagogical prevention.[1]

Now that the civil marriage family in its traditional form enjoys increasingly less societal recognition, the pedagogical concerns that it included must be transposed in one way or another into an institution that is validated by society. People who live together and are planning to have and to bring up children can and must

---

[*] Dr. Hans van Crombrugge is senior researcher at the Higher Institute of Family Sciences, Brussels (www.hig.be), where he teaches foundations of educational theory and family pedagogy. Research focuses on history of pedagogical ideas and on parenting. Email: hans.vancrombrugge@hig.be.
[1] See Proposition 2.

be expected to explicitly and publicly commit themselves to parenthood. To this end, one could introduce the institution of the upbringing pledge.

The upbringing pledge means a pronouncement in favour of a lasting commitment with respect to the child. A public and formal pronouncement cultivates intentions that undoubtedly are present, but these receive added societal value via the pledge made. By pronouncing it, the parents acknowledge the responsibility placed on them by the child. A promise is an obligation.

The pledge affirms that the child has the right to a fundamentally indissoluble relationship with his or her parents. The parents commit themselves to always being available to the child and not to interfere with the relationship with the other parent, whatever the relationship between the partners themselves might be. 'We will be there for you.' 'In good and bad days, we remain the parents of our child.'

When registering the birth or adoption of a child, the parents would formally make an upbringing pledge. This presupposes that the civil and public symbolic character of the declaration is preserved. In the case of remarriage or concluding a cohabitation contract or marriage of partners with children, the upbringing pledge can be pronounced in the presence of all the children involved. In the case of divorce, the upbringing pledge will be reconfirmed by the ex-partners.

The upbringing pledge contains not only a statement of lasting commitment concerning care for the children, but also an explicit declaration of commitment to recognize and implement the rights of the child as a person.

The institution of the upbringing pledge for that matter also affirms the government's responsibility: it must support parents and children. In signing the Convention on the Rights of the Child, states after all have committed themselves to doing everything possible to ensure that children are able to grow up in a dignified way. According to the Convention, this implies (1) that for the full and harmonious development of the child's personality, he or she must grow up in a family environment, in an atmosphere of happiness, love and understanding; (2) that the child is brought up by parents who are recognized in their common responsibility for the upbringing. The government must do all it can to ensure this. Instead of sanctioning parents who appear to fall short in taking up their responsibility (we are thinking here of the proposal to withhold child allowance or a part of a scholarship in the case of school truancy), the government should rather create a positive climate that cultivates commitment. The institution of the upbringing pledge could be a step in the right direction.

2. UPBRINGING PLEDGE AND THE RIGHTS OF THE CHILD: SOME PROPOSITIONS

2.1. THE PEDAGOGICAL RESPONSIBILITY OF THE STATE

Proposition 1
The Convention on the Rights of the Child recognizes the rights of the parents[2] as those with the primary responsibility for the upbringing and development of their child. It also establishes the right of children to common parental care and upbringing in a family environment. In this, the role of the states with respect to the upbringing is also established. In several articles, the convention describes the scope of the secondary responsibility of the states in both general and specific situations. These actions – which we could describe as social-pedagogical action and empowerment – presuppose a more fundamental and foundational anchoring of the secondary responsibility of states: 'State Parties shall use their best efforts to ensure recognition of the principle that both parents have common responsibilities for the upbringing and development of the child.'[3] In our view, this concern for the recognition of this principle also requires 'institutional action', in particular the establishment of the 'upbringing family' by an upbringing pledge.

Proposition 2
Seen in a historical perspective, the civil marriage family was a social institution that regulated more than the life together of two adults. It also had a pedagogical legitimacy and objective: in particular, to ensure that the children resulting from the relationship were cared for and brought up well. The demands placed on the partners who wished to marry were also conditions that candidate parents had to fulfil. In this sense, the civil marriage family was considered an instrument of states to engage in general pedagogical prevention: to ensure that children have parents who will take good care of them. The point of departure and argumentation here was that parents have not only the right and the obligation to care for their own children, but that they as lovers who voluntarily commit to marriage must also have the best pedagogical intentions with respect to the children who result from the marriage. The role of states in this construction is secondary, sup-

---

[2] In the Convention, the term "parents" is used in an undefined (and undifferentiated) way. In the following, the term "parents" does not necessarily refer to the biological father and mother, but rather to all adult persons who enjoy societal and legal recognition as parents of the child by virtue of a biological relationship, adoption and recognition, as well as actual care for the child.
[3] *Convention on the Rights of the Child,* Article 18.1.

plementary and supportive (e.g. providing the material conditions required by the households, increasing parental skills). States only intervene when it appears that the parents are unable to bring up their children properly (e.g. in the case of neglect and abuse).[4]

Proposition 3
Since the civil marriage family in its traditional form enjoys increasingly less societal recognition and validity (due to questionable assumptions regarding the coherence of sexuality, reproduction and upbringing), states cannot limit themselves to noting this decreasing legitimacy and attractiveness. Because of their pedagogical responsibility, states cannot limit themselves to instituting cohabitation contracts in the context of maximizing peoples' freedom of choice with respect to the organization of the partners' intimate life together. In one way or another, the pedagogical concerns that were contained in the institution of the civil marriage family must be translated into an institution that is recognized by society.[5]

2.2. PARENTHOOD

Proposition 4
People who live together and plan to bring up children can and must be expected to explicitly commit themselves to parenthood. Because the child is a human being and citizen, child rearing cannot be considered a private matter. Because the child is a human being and citizen for whom society is responsible, the commitment of child rearers will have a public character.

Proposition 5
The upbringing pledge concerns the pronouncement of a number of fundamental children's rights and the commitment to personally guarantee these rights. In the first place the child has the right to continuous personal care by his or her parents. The parents must affirm that the child has the right to an indissoluble relationship with both parents. They commit themselves to always being available to the child and not to interfere with the relationship with the other parent, whatever the relationship between the partners themselves might be. 'In good days and in bad, we remain the parents of our child'. 'We will be there for you.'

---

[4] This argument is analyzed in: H. Van Crombrugge (20011/1999). *Verwantschap en verschil.* Antwerp: Garant; See also: H. Van Crombrugge & L. Vandemeulebroecke (1993). The child-bearing-childrearing connection. In: J.M. Laboa (Ed.). *Politicas de la familia.* (pp. 629–647). Madrid: Comillias.

[5] For this discussion, comp. D.W. Archard (2003). *Children, family and the state.* Burlington: Ashgate.

Proposition 6

Parents may also be expected to support children's rights. This amounts to no more or no less than voicing the idea that children are persons and must be treated as such, taking into account their uniqueness (as a child and as an individual). Society may expect parents to engage in a process of upbringing in which the children are recognized as discussion partners: as people who have something to say, who are listened to and who can be addressed as persons. This is not to impose a specific concrete model of upbringing on parents. It here concerns a choice in principle for the child, which is translated differently according to the child, his or her developmental stage, the parent and the situation. States that signed the Convention on the Rights of the Child have indeed committed themselves to respecting these rights, not only in public life, but also in all families and for all children.[6]

2.3. SUPPORTING THE PARENTS

Proposition 7

The child has a right to expert parents. This means that parents must be able to 'prove' that they are good parents. It is enough that parents declare that they are prepared to inform themselves as much as possible about children, what their needs are, what they as parents can offer them and the like. Why for that matter would it not be possible to request (future) parents to attend a 'school for parents'. It is clear that we are not speaking here of a real school, but rather of a meeting with other parents in order to reflect on what upbringing is (for them), to ask questions, gather information and to listen to other parents. Effects in terms of more successful upbringing – whatever this might be – cannot be expected. The goal must be to make people aware of the scope and the responsibility of parenthood.[7]

Proposition 8

In its preamble, the Convention on the Rights of the Child very clearly states that 'the child, for the full and harmonious development of his or her personality, should grow up in a family environment, in an atmosphere of happiness, love and

---

[6] The meaning of the Convention on the rights of the child as a 'pedagogical constitution' has been analyzed in: H. Van Crombrugge (1999). De gezinspedagogische betekenis van het Verdrag inzake Rechten van het Kind. In: M. Bouverne-de Bie a.o. *Het gezin en de rechten van het kind.* (pp. 13–58). Leuven-Amersfoort: Acco.

[7] An inspiring example of this kind of Family Life Education is developed by Margaret Sawin – M.S. Sawin (1986). The family cluster approach to family enrichment. In: W. Denton (Ed.). *Marriage and family enrichment.* (pp.47–58). New York: Haworth.

understanding'.⁸ This implies that states cannot avoid establishing what is to be understood by a 'pedagogically valuable family environment'.

Proposition 9
One may object to these proposals as too pedagogically normative, based on a fear of legalizing the parent-child relationship with interventions on the part of the authorities. This concern is misplaced. Legal provisions after all do not relieve the partners in a relationship of their responsibilities. Such provisions rather appear to function as principles to which people can/must orientate themselves when determining what is or is not responsible. There is no need to fear an imminent 'collectivization' of family upbringing. The state must facilitate the support, but not necessarily organize it (and can leave this to private initiatives).⁹

2.4. CONCRETE PROPOSALS

Proposition 10
When registering a child's birth, parents make a formal pledge with respect to upbringing. This presupposes that the civil and public symbolic character of this birth registration is preserved.

Proposition 11
In the case of remarriage or concluding a cohabitation contract or marriage of partners with children, the upbringing pledge must be pronounced in the presence of all the children involved. In the case of divorce, the upbringing pledge must be reconfirmed by the ex-partners.

Proposition 12
The upbringing pledge contains not only a statement of lasting commitment concerning care for the children, but also an explicit declaration of commitment to the recognition and implementation of the rights of the child as prescribed by the Convention on the Rights of the Child.

Proposition 13
In accordance with Article 14 of the Convention on the Rights of the Child and the Universal Declaration of Human Rights, the upbringing pledge ensures par-

---

8   *Convention on the Rights of the Child*, Preambular paragraph 6.
9   For this argument, see: O. O'Neill & W. Ruddick (Eds.). *Having children. Philosophical and Legal reflections on parenthood.* Oxford: Oxford University Press. See also: H. LaFolette (1980). Licensing parents. *Philosophy & Public Affairs*, 9(2), 182–197; L.E. Frisch (1981). On licentious licensing, *Philosophy & Public Affairs*, 11(2), 173–183.

ents the optimum possibilities to raise children in accordance with their own religious and/or philosophical convictions.

3. DISCUSSION

We may assume that most parents want the best for their children. They are prepared to do whatever it takes to ensure the well-being and development of their children. The good intentions of parents also go hand in hand with many questions on the part of parents whether they indeed will be able to bring up the children, whether they are doing the right things and whether they are really capable of bringing the task of upbringing to a good result. Parents know that they are not the only ones engaged in raising their children: numerous other societal influences play an important role. For that matter, not all influences can be controlled by parents. This conclusion, however, does not diminish the responsibility of parents. On the contrary, parents are faced with the task of also taking into consideration these uncontrollable influences and situations and in finding meaningful ways to deal with them and to continue to look for growth opportunities for the children, for themselves and for the relationship with their children. Children did not ask to be born into this world. Parents must organize the world as well as they can to allow the child to develop and discover him or herself. This aspect of parental responsibility is beautifully depicted in the film *La vita è bella*. The father is not responsible for the fact that his child is placed in a labour camp. However, he considers it his responsibility to follow the child in captivity and as much as possible to imaginatively translate for the child everything that occurs into situations that provide growth opportunities for the child. It is his responsibility to make the world 'meaning-ful' for the child.[10]

In the upbringing relationship, the child is an active partner, an active self-willing, meaning giver. The parent or guardian is obliged to allow the child to participate actively in looking for sense and meaning in the world in which he or she lives. The child will often also add elements to the world of the parents. This is the child's right. The child must also gradually learn to assume responsibility for this contribution and for his or her reinterpretation of the world as well as for the way in which the relationship with the parents develops. In this sense, upbringing is searching together for the most meaningful world for all concerned. However, the

---

[10] On the theory of child rearing as an 'aesthetic representation of the world (Herbart)' and possible comments from a critical point of view, see: H. Van Crombrugge (in press). Tussen zin en verstand. Opvoeding als levensbeschouwelijke praktijk. In *Zin in gezin*. Tielt: Lannoo; see also: H. A. Alexander (2001). *Reclaiming goodness. Education and the spiritual quest*. Notre Dame, Indiana: University of Notre Dame Press.

responsibilities of parent and child are not equal. The parent retains the primary responsibility for creating a situation in which children can learn to take up their own responsibility – gradually, according to the development of their capabilities and their experiences. As a person, the child is entitled to recognition as a discussion partner. The child must be listened to and a dialogue must be entered into. However, in order to be recognized as a discussion partner and to engage in dialogue, a person must be taken into a symbolic discourse and receive a name and learn a language. Without a name, the child can never say "I"; without language, the child cannot speak. Giving a name and deciding which language will be spoken with the child are the responsibility of the parents. In this, the child not only has nothing to say, if he or she later has problems due to this (and what is puberty if not the person wrestling with all of these given elements – such as language, name, parents and the like – that one did not choose but that one must integrate and take responsibility for), it is the obligation of the parents to assist the child in resolving these problems.[11]

In short, the fact that there are many influences that the parent does not have under control, that the child influences the parent and that the child must be able to actively participate in his or her upbringing, takes nothing away from this parental responsibility: it does not diminish it, it makes it more complex.[12]

This is not to say that parents are the only ones who are responsible. Equal responsibility attaches to society which is the source of the diverse influences that impact on the child. The government has very important responsibilities. The government must not and cannot fulfil the role of parents, but it must and can support parents in taking up their responsibility. This occurs in many different ways, each of which must be judged on its own merits. We note that the government is increasingly more active in assisting parents and more explicitly assuming responsibility for raising children. There are various causes and circumstances behind this. One factor that should not be underestimated is the Convention on the Rights of the Child. In signing the Convention on the Rights of the Child, the states committed themselves to helping realize the rights of the child in all possible ways. Supporting the parents in raising children is an important element of this. According to these rights of the child, the child not only has the right to parents, but especially the right to good parents. And the convention indeed has a substantial view of what the essential qualities of good upbringing are. Belonging to good upbringing is a relationship with the parents. Belonging to good

---

[11] For this argument, I am inspired by: P. Ricoeur (1990). *Soi-même comme un autre*. Paris: Seuill (especially his discussion with MacIntyre's *After Virue*).

[12] See: H. van Crombrugge (2007). Beschouwingen over de onvermijdelijke en asymetrische verantwoordelijkheid van ouders. In G. Jennes e.a. *Beseffen alle ouders wat verantwoordelijk-zijn voor een kind is?* (pp. 15–24). Brussels/Antwerp: HIG – ROJ.

upbringing is also the recognition of the child as an active participant in his or her own upbringing with a unique position that requires specific protection.

It is incorrect to assert that the convention does not impose a normative model of upbringing on the government. The measures that the government takes and the institutions that the government sets up for this purpose, all imply a well-defined vision of children and upbringing. In this, participation is indeed a central concept. Because of this participation, clear norms can be imposed on the government and parents with respect to assuming their responsibility. For that matter, participation implies normative, communicative ethics, which means that the actions for enlarging the active participation of all concerned in the upbringing are not only supportive, but also normative and regulative. The normative framework of children's rights creates a space in which the subject is still able to develop many of his or her own accents and can have many different convictions concerning what 'good upbringing' is.

Parents may have the best intentions and still have different views of what good upbringing is; in taking up responsibility for the upbringing and development of the relationship with their children, they must be addressed to the extent to which they do justice to the child as a specially placed discussion partner. The government must support them in this task as much as possible, but in so doing is bound by the way in which the Convention on the Rights of the Child interprets this 'image of the child'. As explained, all of this does not diminish the responsibility of the parents, but makes it more complex. In the same way, the responsibility of government is also greater and more complex.[13] And again: this recognition of pedagogical responsibility in no way takes away from the position of the child as a person entitled to active participation. On the contrary, in this model of upbringing, the child is more quickly given increasing responsibility for his or her own upbringing.

All parents need and deserve a great deal of help and support in realizing their good intentions in their own special way, within the space structured by the rights of the child. The societal institution of the upbringing pledge is one of the possible resources to support parents and one of the many resources which is not insignificant and certainly not without benefit. Based on the nature of the upbringing pledge, however, its meaning cannot be articulated in terms of effectiveness or guarantees.

It appears from everything said above that the birth of a child and caring for a child are not private matters. The child, as a person who has a right to recognition

---

[13] Comp. A.L. Alstott (2004). *No exit. What parents owe their children and what society owes parents.* Oxford: Oxford University Press.

of his or her human dignity, engages all of society. There are people who, for all sorts of reasons, are more involved with the child and for whom caring for their well-being and upbringing are, as it were, self-evident (because of affinity or because of affinity on the part of the child with a person with whom one is intimately involved). At an individual level, these people have diverse intentions. Giving people the chance to articulate these intentions before society is not without importance. By articulating personal subjective feelings, these intentions are as it were objectified into actual societal commitment, in several meanings of the word. First, the human person who pronounces these words identifies with what he says. Putting into words causes one to reflect on and give shape to what one feels. By putting something into words, I become aware of what I feel and I become more aware of myself: I am the person saying this. In this, words are not neutral means, but rather they force the person to give personal form to his or her intentions. In this way, it also becomes clear for other people as to what I feel and who I am. The articulation of feelings in itself is often a struggle, not only with what one actually feels, but also with the way in which you come across to the other. Thus, putting something into words is never superfluous and self-evident, but rather a non-evident reflection about oneself and the other. What is said, is said. This also means that a person opens him or herself up to judgment. It is clear to the other that you actually intend to commit yourself to your child. Not only does this create the opportunity to be judged in the future, but in this way, you also appeal to the other and, by extension, to society. 'I want to be there for this child' is both a demand for recognition of this commitment and a demand for the commitment of the other. In the upbringing pledge, parents not only engage themselves, but also society and the government before whom the commitment is pronounced. 'I will be there for you' is also 'I wish to be recognized as the one who will be there for you and in this capacity wish to be recognized as someone who has a right to genuine support in realizing this commitment'. Because of these characteristics, the pronouncement of a pledge in itself already contributes to building up the community.

When people are asked to pronounce the upbringing pledge, this is not a mere formality. Time and space are made available for a witness to express a deep conviction. If parenthood indeed is not self-evident, then it is appropriate to reflect briefly on this, as an individual and society. From this point of view, abolishing the personal birth registration at the city hall before a civil servant in the presence of witnesses is undesirable. By giving form in the pronouncement of the pledge as a formal event, the seriousness of parenthood is underlined. It is entirely possible that feeling the community-founding significance of such ceremonies is no longer self-evident in these post-modern times, but this is precisely an argument for establishing such ceremonies. Society has every interest in the cultivation of suitable words and feelings concerning this living together in society, in which expression is given to that which is really important and worthy.

By connecting the pledge 'I will be there for you' with the normative statements contained in the rights of the child, one is not tied down to the mere application of a model of upbringing imposed by the government. The pledge expresses the desire to give shape to the concern for the well-being and development of the child within the framework created by children's rights. Such a commitment is nothing other than expressing the desire to recognize the child as a person, with everything that this entails. The government commits itself to do everything it can to assist parents in fulfilling this pledge. Both the parent or guardian and the government open themselves up to a judgment concerning their commitment to a dignified relationship with their child.

As said above, the benefit of the upbringing pledge is not to be sought in quantifiable effects (less problems with upbringing). For this, other resources must be employed. On the other hand, the meaning of symbols for the quality of society is underestimated. Symbols help determine the culture and the quality of society. The upbringing pledge indeed is a symbol connected with many existing developments and as an expression thereof, helps to support them. Developments in law allow the regulation of parent-child relationships increasingly to be a question of a freely taken decision. The institution of the (explicit) pledge expresses this. When parents separate/divorce, the principle of co-parenthood applies in Belgium as in many other countries). In the pledge, this principle – used if problems should arise – is already pronounced beforehand. In the case of newly composed families and in other situations, a way must be sought to organize the different parental responsibilities (between biological parents, new partners who must be able to assume responsibility, and so on). The pledge can be an important tool here. In regulating the relationship between biological and foster parents in general, there is a need for institutions that regulate the relationship between children and parents. The pledge does not solve the problems, but it does provide a framework within which to deal with the problems. In this sense, the upbringing pledge must be linked to the establishment of parenthood. Seen from this point of view, it does not take anything away from and is not a threat to marriage. The upbringing pledge is a commemoration and rethinking of the birth registration, in times in which nurturing parenthood can no longer be seen as merely linked to biological parenthood in the context of the civil marriage family.

WHAT MAY PARENTS BE ASKED TO PLEDGE?

The Convention on the Rights of the Child as a Source of Parental Duties and Responsibilities

Jan C.M. Willems*

1. INTRODUCTION

Hans Van Crombrugge's proposal of the upbringing (or parenting) pledge – as substantiated and defended in his contributions to this book – aims at promoting parental awareness and child rearing literacy. As such, it is an example of a child rights-based approach to parenting. Such an approach combines two elements: empowerment of (future) parents, and their so-called responsibilization. Empowerment means: facilitating, uniting (bringing young parents together, facilitating organizations of parents), educating, supporting, assisting, listening to and guiding parents, providing leadership to parents, and holding them accountable. Responsibilization means: legislating child rights-based parental responsibilities – basically legislating what is in the Convention on the Rights of the Child (CRC).[1] In other words, responsibilization is about making CRC parental responsibilities part and parcel of national family law, turning international children's rights into crystal clear national parental duties – and holding parents accountable in relation to these duties.[2] In this, but also in other respects, empowerment and respon-

---

* Prof. Dr. Jan C.M. Willems teaches human rights and rights of the child at Maastricht University, and is chair holder of the first (and only) Dutch Chair of Children's Rights at VU University Amsterdam. His research focuses on child rights, secure attachment and prosocial development. Email: j.willems@ir.unimaas.nl.
[1] UN General Assembly 20 November 1989. Text available at <www2.ohchr.org/english/law/crc.htm>.
[2] In this contribution, "duties" refer to legal obligations, either explicitly formulated in national law or generally accepted to be implied in comprehensive legal obligations such as parental authority, c.q. parental responsibility, being the duty and the right of the parent to care for and raise his or her minor child (cf. Dutch Civil Code Article 1:247 para 1). "Responsibilities" refer

sibilization overlap. Both may be seen as elements of psychological emancipation – emancipation through law and education. Both are crucial. One needs the law to educate people on the law: to educate children and adults on child rights and on the parental responsibilities and duties based on those rights and translated into national law. But not only legislation is needed. Investments are needed in all kinds of parent and child facilities and services. And parents need to be educated as well on the availability of programmes and services, on what may and what must be asked from all kinds of professionals – doctors, teachers, social workers, therapists, youth care professionals and so forth. Empowerment begins with education, but it includes many other things, such as child care and early childhood services, counselling, psychotherapy, mediation, and many other forms of both material and immaterial support and assistance.[3]

1.1. TRANSISM

Being an example, and, in my opinion, a very interesting and promising one, of a child rights based approach to parenting, Van Crombrugge's proposal of the upbringing pledge may be seen as falling within the overall child rights' agenda of fighting transism. Transism, or transgenerational discrimination, refers to a state not adequately addressing socio-economic and, more specifically, socio-emotional differences between (young) parents. Socio-economic differences refer to extreme inequalities between (young) parents in relation to income and income-related time – time parents can devote to their children and to child rearing. Socio-emotional differences refer to extreme inequalities between (young) parents in relation to parenting knowledge ("child rearing literacy") and parental awareness, which includes qualities and conditions such as parents' sense of responsibility, parents' responsiveness and sensitivity to their child's needs, parents' reparation of own childhood trauma, parents' mental health, emotional stability and maturity, social network, social integration, and so forth. By not or not adequately addressing these inequalities states contribute to widespread transgenerational transmission of poor mental health or other forms of emotional pov-

---

to pre-legal or quasi-legal ("moral") duties, which may be justiciable under specific or exceptional circumstances only. In other words, duties may be seen as hard law, responsibilities as soft law. It is not always possible, however, to clearly distinguish between the two. On "duties" versus "responsibilities" see also Vandenhole's chapter in this book.

[3] For further elaboration, and several proposals in relation to empowerment and responsibilization, as well as constitutionalization, see my four chapters in JAN C.M. WILLEMS (ed.), *Developmental and Autonomy Rights of Children; Empowering Children, Caregivers and Communities*, Antwerp-Oxford, Intersentia, 2007 (second edition), 65–210.

erty, of poor parenting and of social – socio-emotional and related socio-economic – exclusion.[4]

Announcing Report Card No. 8 on Early Childhood Development, the UNICEF Innocenti Research Centre states:[5]

> "A considerable body of evidence points to the importance of the early years as a window of opportunity to make a difference in the lives of children and to break the intergenerational cycle of poverty [of both socio-economic and socio-emotional poverty, that is, to eliminate transism, JW]. Recognizing this evidence, many countries of the Organisation for Economic Co-operation and Development (OECD) have national strategies for enhancing the experiences of young children. Report Card No. 8 will analyse these countries' response to families and young children, notably in the area of early childhood care and education. OECD governments invest public resources in early childhood services. However, from the point of view of the best interests of the child, the situation in many OECD countries leaves room for improvement and requires a doubling of resources."

The UNICEF Innocenti Research Centre thus points at the need for a "doubling" of resources. Independent experts who operate within the UN framework also stress the importance of early childhood care and education and, more specifically, of preparation for parenthood and parent (that is, parenthood and parenting) education, in order to contribute to the worldwide elimination of transism. The independent monitoring body of the CRC, the Committee on the Rights of the Child, observes in its General Comment No. 5:[6]

> "(…) The Convention [on the Rights of the Child] highlights the importance of the family in its preamble and in many articles. It is particularly important that the promotion of children's rights should be integrated into preparation for parenthood and parenting education."

And in the UN Secretary-General's Study on Violence Against Children it is stated by the Study's independent expert Paulo Sérgio Pinheiro:[7]

---

[4] On the concept of transism, see WILLEMS (ed.), *Developmental and Autonomy Rights of Children* (note 3). On state responsibility and accountability in relation to transism (transgenerational state responsibility), see JAN C.M. WILLEMS, *Wie zal de Opvoeders Opvoeden? Kindermishandeling en het Recht van het Kind op Persoonswording [Who will Educate the Educators? Child Abuse and the Right of the Child to Become a Person]* (with a summary in English), The Hague, T.M.C. Asser Press, 1999, 629–991.
[5] UNICEF Innocenti Research Centre, at <www.unicef-irc.org>, visited 17 March 2008.
[6] Committee on the Rights of the Child, General Comment No. 5 (2003), *General measures of implementation for the Convention on the Rights of the Child*, para 54. Text available at <www.unhchr.ch/tbs/doc.nsf/(symbol)/CRC.GC.2003.5.En?OpenDocument>.
[7] UN Secretary-General's Study on Violence Against Children (2006), para 110. Text available at <www.violencestudy.org/IMG/pdf/English-2-2.pdf>.

"Bearing in mind that the family has the primary responsibility for the upbringing and development of the child and that the State should support parents and caregivers to care for children, I recommend that States: (a) Develop or enhance programmes to support parents and other carers in their child-rearing role. Investments in health care, education and social welfare services should include quality early childhood development programmes, home visitation, pre- and post-natal services and income-generation programmes for disadvantaged groups; (…) (c) Develop gender-sensitive parent education programmes focusing on non-violent forms of discipline. Such programmes should promote healthy parent-child relationships and orient parents towards constructive and positive forms of discipline and child development approaches, taking into account children's evolving capacities and the importance of respecting their views."

Against this broad background of investment and empowerment, the child rights' basis of responsibilization may be further investigated.

1.2. A LIST OF RESPONSIBILITIES

One of the elements of the upbringing pledge is the list of children's rights parents pledge to observe and devote themselves to. In order to draw up such a list, the first question should be: what does the CRC say about parental responsibilities? Or, to put it more concretely, which child rights in the CRC may be seen, or construed, as explicit or rather implied parental responsibilities? In this contribution, I will submit such a list, which is neither meant to be exhaustive, nor meant to be fully incorporated in the pledge, nor in national family law, for that matter. It may be seen, however, as a first step towards drawing up a list of essential parental responsibilities which should be in the law, and may be included in the pledge. Some of the responsibilities in the list are already duties in the national law of some or many states. Some may never be legislated, nor need be. Some should be legislated as a matter of urgency, such as non-violent discipline – as a much needed framework for education on positive parenting[8] and positive discipline.[9] The list may also be seen as a starting point for creating a tool for child rights education on parental duties and responsibilities in schools and elsewhere. Before the list is submitted (in paragraph 3), we will have a closer look at state obligations in the

---

[8] On which see Recommendation (2006)19 of the Committee of Ministers to [Council of Europe] Member States on policy to support positive parenting (Adopted by the Committee of Ministers on 13 December 2006), <www.coe.int>, Institutions/Committee of Ministers, Documents/Adopted texts, Recommendations of the Committee of Ministers to Member States, All Recommendations.

[9] On which see JOAN E. DURRANT, *Positive Discipline: What it is and how to do it*, 2007, online <http://seap.savethechildren.se/South_East_Asia/Misc/Puffs/Positive-Discipline-What-it-is-and-how-to-do-it>.

CRC in the child-parent-state relationship (in paragraph 2). A brief conclusion will end this contribution.

2. STATE EMPOWERMENT AND RESPONSIBILIZATION OBLIGATIONS

Article 3 para 2 of the Convention on the Rights of the Child (CRC) establishes a *Trias pedagogica* of children, parents and the state.[10] It reads as follows:

> Article 3 para 2 – State Parties undertake to ensure the child such protection and care as is necessary for his or her well-being, taking into account the rights and duties of his or her parents, legal guardians, or other individuals legally responsible for him or her, and, to this end, shall take all appropriate legislative and administrative measures.

This paragraph is preceded by the articulation, in Article 3 para 1, of the best interests of the child as a prioritized principle in international (child rights) law. This paragraph reads as follows:

> Article 3 para 1 – In all actions concerning children, whether undertaken by public or private social welfare institutions, courts of law, administrative authorities or legislative bodies, the best interests of the child shall be a primary consideration.

In Article 18 para 1, where the best interests of the child is linked to parental responsibility, the wording appears to be even stronger. This paragraph reads as follows:

> Article 18 para 1 – State Parties shall use their best efforts to ensure recognition of the principle that both parents have common responsibilities for the upbringing and development of the child. Parents or, as the case may be, legal guardians, have the primary responsibility for the upbringing and development of the child. The best interests of the child will be their basic concern.

The best interests of the child, therefore, are concerns of both the state (Article 3 para 1) and parents (Article 18 para 1). According to the whole concept of children's rights, and especially according to Article 12: child participation as a general principle, the child is also an actor in his or her own best interests, that is, in his or her own healthy holistic (that is, physical-emotional-social-moral-intellectual) development, including the pursuit of the other pedagogical aims of the

---

[10] On the concept of the Trias pedagogica, see WILLEMS (ed.), *Developmental and Autonomy Rights of Children* (note 3).

Convention, mentioned – strictly speaking in relation to school education only – in Article 29 para 1. This paragraph reads as follows:

> Article 29 para 1 – State Parties agree that the education of the child shall be directed to:
> (a) The development of the child's personality, talents and mental and physical abilities to their fullest potential;
> (b) The development of respect for human rights and fundamental freedoms, and for the principles enshrined in the Charter of the United Nations;
> (c) The development of respect for the child's parents, his or her own cultural identity, language and values, for the national values of the country in which the child is living, the country from which he or she may originate, and for civilisations different from his or her own;
> (d) The preparation of the child for responsible life in a free society, in the spirit of understanding, peace, tolerance, equality of sexes, and friendship among all peoples, ethnic, national and religious groups and persons of indigenous origin;
> (e) The development of respect for the natural environment.

Taken together, the aims enumerated sub (a) and sub (b)-(e), respectively, may be summarized as holistic development and preparation for democratic citizenship. And the latter may be construed – on the basis, *inter alia*, of Article 18 para 1 (primary responsibility of parents for the development of the child), and Article 29 para 1 sub (d) (preparation of the child for responsible life) – as including preparation for responsible parenthood. Thus, three actors are involved in child development: the state (through its agents and through its responsibilities towards institutions and professionals[11]), parents, and the child himself or herself. All these actors have rights, duties and responsibilities, which, according to their fundamental character, should be constitutionalized, but at any rate should be specified – and clarified – in the national legal system.

2.1. STATE OBLIGATIONS

Two of the most outstanding state obligations, in my opinion, in the CRC are to be found in Article 27 para 3, and Article 18 para 2, which require the state to empower, that is to facilitate, educate, assist and support parents, in socio-economic and socio-emotional ways, respectively. Article 27 reads as follows:

---

[11] On which see Article 3 para 3 CRC: State Parties shall ensure that the institutions, services and facilities responsible for the care or protection of children shall conform with the standards established by competent authorities, particularly in the areas of safety, health, in the number and suitability of their staff, as well as competent supervision.

> Article 27 para 1 – State Parties recognise the right of every child to a standard of living adequate for the child's physical, mental, spiritual, moral and social development.
> 2. The parent(s) or others responsible for the child have the primary responsibility to secure, within their abilities and financial capacities, the conditions of living necessary for the child's development.
> 3. States Parties, in accordance with national conditions and within their means, shall take appropriate measures to assist parents and others responsible for the child to implement this right and shall in case of need provide material assistance and support programmes, particularly with regard to nutrition, clothing and housing.

And Article 18 para 2 states:

> Article 18 para 2 – For the purpose of guaranteeing and promoting the rights set forth in the present Convention, State Parties shall render appropriate assistance to parents and legal guardians in the performance of their child-rearing responsibilities and shall ensure the development of institutions, facilities and services for the care of children.

Specifying and clarifying parental duties and responsibilities, as they appear in the CRC, is also a very important state responsibility, however. Such a specification and clarification provide us with an essential yardstick for parenthood education in schools and parenting education for parents and parents-to-be. As such, they are an integral part of preparation for parenthood and empowerment of children, parents and other carers and the community (neighbours, relatives, professionals, volunteers, bystanders, etc.). Therefore, specification and clarification of parental duties and responsibilities should be considered as an implied state obligation. Furthermore, it may be argued that specifying and clarifying parental duties falls within the scope of the "appropriate legislative and administrative measures" called for by Article 3 para 2, to ensure the child's care and protection with positive regard to parental duties. Responsibilization is the term I use to denote, *inter alia*, the state's obligation to specify and clarify parental duties and responsibilities in the national legal system. The combination of CRC provisions and state obligations mentioned above enables us to present the following definition of (a child rights-based) *Trias pedagogica*.

2.2. TRIAS PEDAGOGICA

Trias pedagogica means the national or constitutional relationship between the state, parents and children, based on children's rights and other human rights and, therefore, implying state obligations in relation to the healthy holistic development of children, including the participation of the child and his or her preparation for democratic citizenship and responsible parenthood, and, more specifically, to the responsibilization and empowerment of parents and other caregivers, professional and otherwise.

Even though the CRC may not make it possible to exactly define the concept of responsible parenthood, it does stipulate the core conditions that have to be met by parents and the state. Apart from CRC Article 18 para 2, and Article 27 para 3 (and a few other provisions), however, it does so in a rather implicit way. Most implicit, of course, are the conditions that have to be distilled out of the principle of the best interests of the child. Let us first have a look at empowerment obligations of states, and then return to parental duties and responsibilities.

2.3. EMPOWERMENT OBLIGATIONS

The following empowerment Articles, divided into two sections (A and B, relating to parents and to children as parents-to-be, respectively), may be discerned in the CRC. This "empowerment list" should not be seen as exhaustive. Also, it should be kept in mind that the state has several obligations which indirectly empower parents, for instance in relation to health care (Article 24), education (Articles 28 and 29), quality of institutions and supervision of professionals (Article 3 para 3), the mass media (Article 17), children's play, sport and cultural activities (Article 31), disabled children (Article 23), foster care (Article 20), and so forth and so on.

Empowerment Articles (A): the state's positive obligations to facilitate, educate, assist and support parents.

- Article 18 para 2 contains the obligation of the state to provide parenting assistance (assistance in the performance of child rearing responsibilities) and support (institutions, facilities and services for the care of children).
- Article 18 para 3, in conjunction with Article 3 para 3, contains the obligation of the state to provide sufficient and high-quality child care services and facilities.
- Article 24 para 2 sub (d)-(f) contains the obligation of the state to provide prenatal and postnatal care, to provide information, education and support for parents, children and all others on child health and nutrition, breastfeeding, hygiene, etc., and to develop preventive health care, guidance for parents and family planning education and services.
- Article 27 para 3 (in conjunction with para 1) contains the obligation of the state to provide material (financial, fiscal and other) assistance and support

for parents so that families may have a standard of living adequate for the child's holistic development.
- Article 27 para 3, in conjunction with Article 18 para 1 (both parents are responsible) and para 2 (parenting assistance), imply a state obligation to (at least) facilitate paid parental leave.

Empowerment Articles (B): the state's positive obligations to empower children as citizens and parents-to-be.

- Article 29 para 1 contains the obligation of the state to see to it that school education be directed to the holistic development of the child and his or her preparation for democratic citizenship (including, as indicated above, responsible parenthood).
- Article 31 para 2 contains the obligation of the state to promote child participation in cultural, recreational and leisure activities.
- Article 39 contains the obligation of the state to promote child trauma reparation (and thus prevent transgenerational transmission of trauma and end cycles of violence, insecure attachment, poor mental health, child abuse and neglect, delinquency,[12] etc.).

In relation to the empowerment list above, it is important to highlight three CRC Articles, namely Article 3 para 3, containing the obligation of the state to empower, that is, to ensure the quantity and quality of, and to supervise institutions and professionals working with parents and/or children; and Article 4 and Article 6 para 2, containing the obligation of the state to invest in children's rights and child development to the maximum extent of its resources. We will now turn to the "responsibilization list": a list of fifty-plus parental duties and responsibilities.

3. FIFTY-PLUS-ONE PARENTAL DUTIES AND RESPONSIBILITIES

The following responsibilization Articles, and ("fifty-plus-one") parental duties and responsibilities to be legislated and/or made known – through information

---

[12] According to TEKIN and CURRIE (ERDAL TEKIN & JANET CURRIE, Does child abuse cause crime?; Abstract, April 2006, available at <papers.ssrn.com/sol3/papers.cfm?abstract_id=895178>), child maltreatment "approximately doubles the probability of engaging in many types of crime. Low SES [socio-economic status, JW] children are both more likely to be mistreated and suffer more damaging effects. Boys are at greater risk than girls, at least in terms of increased propensity to commit crime. Sexual abuse appears to have the largest negative effects (…). Finally, the probability of engaging in crime increases with the experience of multiple forms of maltreatment (…).".

campaigns and education – by the state on the basis of these Articles, may be discerned in the CRC. This list, rather long as it may appear to be, should not be seen as exhaustive, however. It should also be kept in mind that the degree of specification and the details of clarification in national legislation are subject to national democratic process and discretion. In order to enable the reader to compare the list to (short) lists drawn up by specialists from other fields, two alternative lists, one by a mental health specialist and one by a psychologist (containing both parental responsibilities and rights), are included in the appendices to this contribution.

Article 18 para 1 CRC contains three closely related parental duties[13]:
- 1. *both* parents (c.q. caregivers, whatever their gender and marital status) have *common* responsibilities for the upbringing and development of the child;
- 2. parents have the *primary* responsibility for the upbringing and development of the child;
- 3. the best interests of the child will be their *basic concern*. The "best interests" principle consists of fourteen conditions, one of which consists of six sub-conditions (pedagogical model of Margrite Kalverboer & Elianne Zijlstra, 2006).[14] Based on this model, parents have the duty:
- 3.1 to provide physical security;
- 3.2 to provide physical care;
- 3.3 to provide loving care and emotional security;
- 3.4 to provide a supportive and flexible pedagogical structure (in CRC terminology: "direction and guidance consistent with the child's evolving capacities"), for which six sub-conditions have to be met:
- 3.4.1 regularity (so-called routines, rituals and rules);
- 3.4.2 realistic demands (stimulating and instructing the child based on realistic demands);
- 3.4.3 room (to experience, experiment and negotiate);
- 3.4.4 responsibilities (participation in family and community responsibilities);
- 3.4.5 rules (boundaries or limits, which are explained to the child); and

---

[13] In this list, "duty" or "duties" is used as shorthand for duty (duties) and/or responsibility (responsibilities) as defined earlier (note 2).

[14] On this model, see WILLEMS (ed.), *Developmental and Autonomy Rights of Children* (note 3), Chapter 7, at 199–201. The original model is described in Dutch (MARGRITE KALVERBOER & ELIANNE ZIJLSTRA, *Het belang van het kind in het Nederlands recht; Voorwaarden voor ontwikkeling vanuit een pedagogisch perspectief*, Amsterdam, SWP, 2006). However, several elements of the best interests of the child concept are enumerated and elaborated in the Council of Europe recommendation mentioned in note 8 above, as well as in the Explanatory Report to the recommendation (<www.coe.int>, CM(2006)194 add 27 November 2006). Both are included in MARY DALY (ed.), *Parenting in contemporary Europe: A positive approach*, Strasbourg, Council of Europe Publishing, 2007, 141–175.

- 3.4.6 supervision;
- 3.5 to provide continuity in child rearing;
- 3.6 to give personal attention to each individual child;
- 3.7 to set good examples;
- 3.8 to see to their child's education (school, vocational training including sports, music, etc.);
- 3.9 to see to their child's physical and emotional security in school and the community;
- 3.10 to stimulate their child's interaction with peers;
- 3.11 to stimulate their child's access to a social support network;
- 3.12 to devote themselves to active respect for (the human dignity, personal integrity and equal developmental opportunities of) children in school, the community and society;
- 3.13 to contribute to good adult examples in the community and society;
- 3.14 to contribute to stable living conditions in the community and society.

Taken together (and in conjunction with the ninth preambular paragraph), these duties imply a fourth duty:
- 4. both parents have to prepare themselves and actively seek information and support from family, the community and the state before their child is born. Prenatal and perinatal (preparation, c.q. preparation and reparation) responsibilities include:
- 4.1 a physically and mentally healthy lifestyle (*cf.* ninth preambular paragraph and Article 24);
- 4.2 a healthy, stable relationship (*cf.* ninth preambular paragraph and Article 18 para 1);
- 4.3 a stable family income (*cf.* ninth preambular paragraph and Article 27 para 2);
- 4.4 parenting education (*cf.* ninth preambular paragraph and Article 18 para 1, and Article 24);
- 4.5 mental health counselling (own childhood trauma reparation, psychotherapy; *cf.* ninth preambular paragraph and Article 18 para 1, Article 19 para 1, and Article 24).

Article 5, in conjunction with the sixth preambular paragraph, contains the duty of parents:
- 5. to provide affection-based direction and guidance, consistent with the child's evolving capacities (*cf.* 3.4 above).

This duty implies the duty:
- 6. to acquire knowledge on child rearing and child development in general, and

- 7. to seek specific information, advice, feedback and counselling on the rearing and development of their child.

It may even imply the duty:
- 8. to seek psychotherapy in case of relational or psychological problems, or unresolved childhood trauma of the parents themselves.

Article 27 para 2 (in conjunction with para 1) contains the duty of parents:
- 9. to provide a standard of living adequate for the holistic development of their child.

If this is not "within their abilities and financial capacities" (Article 27 para 2), another duty is implied, namely:
- 10. to actively seek family, community and state assistance (cf. Article 27 para 3).

It may also imply the (civic) duty:
- 11. to mobilize parents' organizations, trade unions, child rights NGOs, political parties and the media with a view to improving parenting allowances, benefits and credits.

Taken together, Article 18 para 1 (*both* parents; child's best interests basic concern) and Article 27 para 2 contain the duty of parents:
- 12. to prudently combine work and care, and seek high-quality child care services.

This duty implies the (civic) duty:
- 13. to mobilize parents' organizations, trade unions, child rights NGOs, political parties and the media if national policies are lacking or inadequate in this regard.

Article 19 para 1, in conjunction with General Comment No. 8,[15] contains the duty of parents:
- 14. not to use any form of violence, including humiliation, in child rearing.

This duty implies the duty:
- 15. to acquire knowledge on positive parenting[16] and non-violent child rearing (positive discipline[17]), and
- 16. to seek advice, feedback and counselling if this causes any problems or difficulties.

---

[15] Committee on the Rights of the Child, General Comment No. 8 (2006), *The right of the child to protection from corporal punishment and other cruel or degrading forms of punishment*. Text available at <www.unhchr.ch/tbs/doc.nsf/(Symbol)/CRC.C.GC.8.En?OpenDocument>.
[16] See note 8.
[17] See note 9.

Article 24 para 1, in conjunction with Article 39, contains the duty of parents:
- 17. to seek the best available physical and mental health care for their child.

This duty implies the (civic) duty:
- 18. to mobilize parents' organizations, trade unions, child rights NGOs, political parties and the media, or to go to court, if health care is lacking or inadequate.

Article 24 para 3 contains the duty of parents:
- 19. not to resort to and to abandon any harmful child rearing practices and traditions.

This duty implies the (civic) duty:
- 20. to mobilize parents' organizations, trade unions, child rights NGOs, political parties and the media if the state is not doing enough to ban such practices and to support parents in child rights-based parenting and positive discipline.

Article 28 para 1 contains the duty of parents:
- 21. to send their child to school and see to their child's education and vocational training.

This duty implies the (civic) duty:
- 22. to mobilize parents' organizations, trade unions, child rights NGOs, political parties and the media, or to go to court, if schools are lacking or school education is inadequate.

Article 29 para 1, in conjunction with the seventh preambular paragraph, as well as in conjunction with Article 18 para 1, and Article 19 para 1, contains the duty of parents:
- 23. not to harm and confuse their child, and compromise his or her loyalty, by raising him or her contrary to the CRC's holistic development and democratic and cosmopolitan citizenship aims of education.

Article 17 contains the two-sided duty of parents:
- 24. to stimulate the child's use of media that contribute to his or her holistic development and physical and mental health, including his or her democratic and cosmopolitan citizenship education; and
- 25. to protect the child from harmful material.

These duties imply the (civic) duty:
- 26. to mobilize parents' organizations, trade unions, child rights NGOs, political parties and the media themselves if the state and/or the media are not meeting the standards of Article 17.

Article 30 in conjunction with Article 29 contains the duty of parents who belong to an ethnic, religious or linguistic minority:
- 27. to promote their child's and their family's integration in society on the basis of their own cultural identity.

Article 31 para 1, in conjunction with Article 18 para 1, and Article 24, contains the duty of parents:
- 28. to provide age-appropriate play and recreational and cultural activities for their child.

This duty implies the (civic) duty:
- 29. to mobilize parents' organizations, trade unions, child rights NGOs, political parties and the media if national policies or community facilities in this respect are lacking or inadequate.

Article 7 para 1 contains two duties of parents:
- 30. to register their child at birth, and
- 31. to inform their child about his or her biological origins.

Article 8 para 1 contains the duty of parents:
- 32. not to deprive their child of his or her personal identity (the knowledge of his or her origins).

Article 9 para 3 contains the two-sided duty of divorced or separated parents:
- 33. to enable their child to maintain personal relations and direct contact with both parents on a regular basis, and
- 34. to prevent contact if it is contrary to the child's best interests.

Article 2 in conjunction with Article 18 para 1 contains the duty of parents:
- 35. not to discriminate between boy and girl children, and
- 36. not to favour one child above the other.

Article 12, in conjunction with Article 18 para 1, and Articles 5 and 29, contains the duty of parents:
- 37. to stimulate their child to form his or her own views and to freely express himself or herself, and
- 38. to stimulate their child, and to provide direction and guidance in this respect, to bear his or her own responsibilities in family, school, the community and country.

Article 13, in conjunction with Article 18 para 1, and Articles 5, 17 and 36, contains the duty of parents:

- 39. to respect and promote their child's freedom of expression and freedom to seek, receive and impart information and ideas, and to provide direction, guidance and protection in this respect.

Article 14 para 1, in conjunction with Article 18 para 1, and Articles 5, 14 para 2, 17 and 36, contains the duty of parents:
- 40. to respect and promote their child's freedom of thought, conscience and religion, and to provide direction, guidance and protection in this respect.

Article 15, in conjunction with Article 18 para 1, and Articles 5, 17 and 36, contains the duty of parents:
- 41. to respect and promote their child's freedom of association and peaceful assembly, and to provide direction, guidance and protection in this respect.

Article 16 in conjunction with Article 18 para 1 contains the duty of parents:
- 42. to respect their child's privacy and personal integrity.

Article 20 para 3, in conjunction with Article 18 para 1, and Article 24, contains the duty of parents:
- 43. to seek foster care or adoption if they are unable to raise their child themselves.

Article 23, in conjunction with Article 18 para 1, and Article 24, contains the duty of parents:
- 44. to seek special care and opportunities for their physically, mentally and/or emotionally disabled child.

This duty implies the (civic) duty:
- 45. to mobilize parents' organizations, trade unions, child rights NGOs, political parties and the media if national policies or community facilities in this respect are lacking or inadequate.

Article 32, in conjunction with Article 18 para 1, and Article 24, contains the duty of parents:
- 46. to stimulate their child to work for as many hours as – and to prevent their child from working for more hours than – are beneficial for his or her holistic development.

Article 33, in conjunction with Article 18 para 1, and Article 24, contains the duty of parents:
- 47. to prevent their child (in cooperation and coordination with other parents and social partners) from smoking, using illegal drugs and abusing alcohol.

Article 34, in conjunction with Articles 17, 18 para 1, 24 and 29, contains the duty of parents:
- 48. to see to their child's sexual education and to prevent their child (in cooperation and coordination with other parents and social partners) from falling victim to sexual exploitation and sexual abuse by peers, predators and paedophiles.

Article 36, in conjunction with Articles 17, 18 para 1, 24 and 29, contains the duty of parents:
- 49. to see to their child's financial, consumer and "screen" or "electronic" (TV, PC, MSN, video games, internet, mobiles, etc.) education and to prevent their child from falling victim to commercial, "electronic" and any other exploitation.

This duty implies the (civic) duty:
- 50. to mobilize parents' organizations, trade unions, child rights NGOs, political parties and the media if national policies are lacking or inadequate in this regard.

Article 42 in conjunction with Article 18 para 1, and Article 29 contains the duty of parents:
- 51. to educate their child on his or her rights and to see to their child's child rights education in school (and the community).

4. CONCLUSION

In his contributions to this book, Van Crombrugge goes into large detail about how and when, by whom and in whose presence, the upbringing pledge may be taken. In this contribution we turned to the Convention on the Rights of the Child to see what may be the actual content, in whole or in part, of such a pledge. We distilled some fifty-one parental responsibilities from the CRC's principles and provisions. Some of these are already part of family law in some or many states; others are still awaiting state legislative action. Most of them are implied – or may be considered to be implied – in the overall parental duty-and-right to raise one's child, in the way the law defines parental responsibility, parental care or parental authority. The list may be seen as a first step towards drawing up a list of essential parental responsibilities which should be in the law, and may be included in the pledge. The list may also be seen as a starting point for creating a tool for child rights education on parental duties and responsibilities in schools and elsewhere.

Maybe pedagogues and psychologists[18] could be invited to join efforts with child rights academics and activists to use the list to create a "top ten" of caregivers' duties and to draw up a version of the upbringing pledge containing essential child rights-based parental responsibilities.

APPENDIX 1. EIGHT ESSENTIAL PARENTAL RESPONSIBILITIES

by CHRIS THEISEN[19]

<www.familyresource.com/parenting/parent-education/8-essential-parental-responsibilities> (visited 28 March 2008)

Introduction
Nobody ever said that children were easy to raise. They don't come with guidelines or instructions and they certainly don't come with a *pause* button (...). What they do come with is a crucial set of physical and emotional needs that must be met. Failure of the parents to meet these specific needs can have wide-ranging and long-lasting negative effects.

The following outline provides eight essential responsibilities that parents must adhere to in order to foster their child's physical and/or emotional well-being:

1. **Provide an environment that is SAFE**
   - Keep your child free from physical, sexual and emotional abuse.
   - Keep unsafe objects locked up or out of reach of your child.
   - Get to know your child's caregivers (get references or background checks).
   - Correct any potential dangers around the house.
   - Take safety precautions: use smoke and carbon monoxide detectors, lock doors at night, always wear seatbelts, etc.

---

[18] See also the two alternative lists, one by a mental health specialist and one by a psychologist, which are included in the appendices below.
[19] Chris Theisen is a Mental Health Specialist who earned his degree from the University of Northern Colorado in 1994. Since then he has spent over 10 years working directly with children who have been diagnosed with such problems as: ADHD, bipolar disorder, conduct disorder, oppositional-defiant disorder, PTSD and autism. He is the author of the Parent Coach plan (<www.parentcoachplan.com>). The Parent Coach plan was developed through a combination of Chris's experience with these children and the effects that he has seen by using behaviour management programmes in various facilities where he has worked.

2. Provide your child with BASIC NEEDS
   - Water
   - Plenty of nutritious foods
   - Shelter
   - A warm bed with sheets, blankets and a pillow
   - Medical care as needed/Medicine when ill
   - Clothing that is appropriate for the weather conditions
   - Space (a place where he or she can go to be alone)

3. Provide your child with SELF-ESTEEM NEEDS
   - Accept your child's uniqueness and respect his or her individuality.
   - Encourage (don't push) your child to participate in a club, activity or sport.
   - Notice and acknowledge your child's achievements and pro-social behaviour.
   - Encourage proper hygiene (to look good is to feel good …).
   - Set expectations for your child that are realistic and age-appropriate.
   - Use your child's misbehaviour as a time to teach, not to criticize or ridicule.

4. Teach your child MORALS and VALUES
   - Honesty
   - Respect
   - Responsibility
   - Compassion
   - Patience
   - Forgiveness
   - Generosity

5. Develop MUTUAL RESPECT with your child
   - Use respectful language
   - Respect his or her feelings
   - Respect his or her opinions
   - Respect his or her privacy
   - Respect his or her individuality

6. Provide DISCIPLINE which is effective and appropriate
   - Structured
   - Consistent
   - Predictable
   - Fair

7. Involve yourself in your child's EDUCATION
   - Communicate regularly with your child's teacher(s).
   - Make sure that your child is completing his or her homework each night.

- Assist your child with his or her homework, but don't DO the homework.
- Talk to your child each day about school (what is being studied, any interesting events, etc.).
- Recognize and acknowledge your child's academic achievements.

8. **Get to KNOW YOUR CHILD**
- Spend quality time together.
- Be approachable to your child.
- Ask questions.
- Communicate. Communicate. Communicate.

Eight responsibilities parents do NOT have

Now that we've looked at the responsibilities parents HAVE, let's look at what responsibilities parents do NOT have. The following is a list of responsibilities that no parent should be expected to meet.

1. Supplying your child with the most expensive designer clothes or shoes available.
2. Picking up after your child/cleaning your child's room.
3. Dropping everything you're doing to give your child a ride somewhere.
4. Providing your child with a telephone, television, computer or game system.
5. Bailing your child out of trouble every time he or she does something wrong.
6. Maintaining an unlimited supply of treats, chips, soda or junk food for your child's unlimited consumption.
7. Replacing toys or other items that your child has lost or misplaced.
8. Welcoming any or all of your child's friends into your home for social or other activities.

APPENDIX 2. TEN PARENTAL RESPONSIBILITIES & TEN PARENTAL RIGHTS

From: Dr. Maggie Mamen (psychologist), The pampered child syndrome – and how to avoid it <www.rccdsb.edu.on.ca/jbosco/Dr.%20Maggie%20Mamen%20Presentation.pdf> (visited 28 March 2008)

Ten parental responsibilities

1. To nurture children
2. To keep them safe

3. To provide for their basic needs
4. To build trust, credibility and respect
5. To socialize children
6. To teach moral values
7. To encourage a sense of self
8. To foster a sense of community
9. To be a positive role model
10. To prepare them for real life.

Ten parental rights

1. To be the architects of the family
2. To constitute the management team
3. To set policy and procedures
4. To have a weighted vote
5. To not be verbally, physically or otherwise battered
6. To make choices
7. To make decisions
8. To think before deciding *("If you want an answer now, it's no")*
9. To enjoy our home and family
10. To have adult time.

CHILDREN'S RIGHTS, PARENTAL RESPONSIBILITIES AND STATE OBLIGATIONS: A COUNCIL OF EUROPE PERSPECTIVE

Wouter Vandenhole[*]

Traditionally, human rights primarily organize the relationship between a state and the individuals within its jurisdiction. Children's rights, understood as the human rights of a particular group of individuals, i.e. children, do the same. But the situation is more sophisticated in the context of children's rights, for there is also more explicitly an intermediary level of parents and caregivers.[1] Article 18 of the Convention on the Rights of the Child (CRC) e.g. recognizes that parents or legal guardians have the primary responsibility for the upbringing and development of the child. States are to render appropriate assistance to parents and legal guardians in the performance of their child-rearing responsibilities, as well as to ensure the development of institutions, facilities and services for the care of children. Article 18(1) and (2) CRC reads:

> 1. State Parties shall use their best efforts to ensure recognition of the principle that both parents have common responsibilities for the upbringing and development of the child. Parents or, as the case may be, legal guardians, have the primary responsibility for the upbringing and development of the child. The best interests of the child will be their basic concern.
> 2. For the purpose of guaranteeing and promoting the rights set forth in the present Convention, States Parties shall render appropriate assistance to parents and legal guardians in the performance of their child-rearing responsibilities and shall ensure the development of institutions, facilities and services for the care of children.

---

[*] Professor of human rights law and holder of the UNICEF Chair in Children's Rights, Faculty of Law, University of Antwerp (Belgium).
[1] As Alston has pointed out, the UN Convention on the Rights of the Child, and by extension, children's rights, do not offer a single answer to the division of responsibility (see Ph. ALSTON, "The Best Interests Principle: Towards a Reconciliation of Culture and Human Rights", *International Journal of Law and the Family* 1994, 2).

Article 17(1)(a) of the Revised European Social Charter (RESC) too refers to the duties of parents, albeit in weaker terms, and to the complementary obligations of states to ensure that children and young persons have the care, the assistance, the education and the training they need. Article 17(1)(a) RESC reads:

> With a view to ensuring the effective exercise of the right of children and young persons to grow up in an environment which encourages the full development of their personality and of their physical and mental capacities, the Parties undertake, either directly or in co-operation with public and private organisations, to take all appropriate and necessary measures designed:
> 1 a. to ensure that children and young persons, taking account of the rights and duties of their parents, have the care, the assistance, the education and the training they need, in particular by providing for the establishment or maintenance of institutions and services sufficient and adequate for this purpose;
>   b. to protect children and young persons against negligence, violence or exploitation;
>   c. to provide protection and special aid from the state for children and young persons temporarily or definitively deprived of their family's support;

From the outset, I would like to clarify a general matter of terminology, which is immediately also a clarification of some of the terminology used in the title. Both 'responsibilities' and 'obligations' are referred to. In this chapter, obligations are understood as legally binding; responsibilities are not. Obligations are incumbent upon the state, whereas responsibility may be assigned to both the state and other actors, such as parents, caregivers or legal guardians.

In this chapter, a Council of Europe perspective is taken. Therefore, not so much the CRC, but the European Convention on Human Rights (ECHR) and the (Revised) European Social Charter ((R)ESC) are relied on as the main source of analysis. The European Convention on Human Rights was adopted in 1950. It covers mainly civil and political rights. Supervision of the implementation of the Convention is exercised by the European Court of Human Rights (ECtHR) in Strasbourg, which deals with individual complaints. All 47 member states of the Council of Europe are also State Parties to the ECHR. The European Social Charter was adopted in 1961. It contains economic and social rights. The ESC was amended in 1996. The RESC is gradually replacing the 1961 ESC. The implementation of the (R)ESC is supervised by the European Committee of Social Rights (ECSR) through the examination of state reports and collective complaints. The RESC has been ratified so far by 24 states. All Member States of the Council of Europe have at least signed either the ESC or the RESC.

The (R)ESC has a strong family perspective. Article 17 (R)ESC, which deals with the rights of children to social, legal[2] and economic protection is preceded by Article 16 on the right of the family to social, legal and economic protection. Notwithstanding this strong family perspective, and while taking into account the evolving nature of the family (e.g. the partial demise of marriage), the European Committee of Social Rights has never emphasized the need for an alternative social contract between parents and children, such as an upbringing pledge. The task in this chapter is therefore to explore whether the ECSR has implicitly or indirectly expressed itself on an upbringing pledge or similar initiatives.

In what follows, the human rights of children, the human rights and responsibilities of parents/caregivers, and the obligations of the state will successively be dealt with. This should lead to a clearer framework of the division of responsibility for child rearing between in particular the parents or caregivers, and the state. Subsequently, the work of the Council of Europe in the area of social cohesion will be briefly looked into. In the final part, the question will be answered to what extent children's rights and human rights from a Council of Europe perspective either allow for, support or rather reject an upbringing pledge. It will be concluded that the ECSR neither prohibits nor recommends such a pledge.

1. HUMAN RIGHTS OF CHILDREN

Children's rights are protected in the (R)ESC both through rights for children themselves, and through rights of the family: "As members of a family, young persons are on the one hand protected by provisions relating to the status of the child [...] and on the other hand by the specific measures protecting the family of which they are a member."[3]

Article 16 (R)ESC guarantees the right of the family to social, legal and economic protection. It reads:

> With a view to ensuring the necessary conditions for the full development of the family, which is a fundamental unit of society, the Parties undertake to promote the economic, legal and social protection of family life by such means as social and family benefits, fiscal arrangements, provision of family housing, benefits for the newly married and other appropriate means.

No definition of family has been provided by either the Charter or the European Committee of Social Rights, but there is clearly an awareness within the ECSR of

---

[2] Only in the RESC.
[3] ECSR, *Conclusions* XIII-2 (General Introduction), para. 60.

changing social perceptions and attitudes towards the family and roles within the family. The Committee has recognized explicitly that the nuclear family, consisting of married parents and their children, has been modified by factors such as a rising divorce rate, social and legal recognition of cohabitation, and the prevalence of so-called broken homes and reconstituted families. Single families are therefore also covered[4] and the notion of family is not restricted to family based on marriage: every constellation defined as family by national law falls under the protection of Article 16.[5]

Also, it has been acknowledged that the traditional organization of the family and the role assigned to individuals within the family has changed enormously, as a consequence of *inter alia* economic changes and the promotion of gender equality.[6] The Committee nevertheless deals rather carefully with these developments, in that it "take[s] into account the evolving nature of the family, but [is] not expecting more of contracting parties than the existing European consensus would permit."[7]

The purpose of the right to protection of families is to give scope to the individual(s) belonging to a family, rather than to remedy a need.[8] Developments in family organization have changed the requirements for protection.[9] Article 16 has therefore been given a dynamic interpretation. Illustrations of this dynamic interpretation can be found in the issue of parental leave[10] and of the rights of single parent families. The latter have been argued to be in need of special protection in terms of family benefits.[11] Under Article 17 ESC too, questions have been asked concerning single parents, without distinguishing between mothers and fathers, although the provision is strictly speaking confined to the protection of mothers (and children).[12]

---

[4] See Appendix to the RESC, Article 16.
[5] See ECSR, *Digest of the Case Law* 2006 (Article 16), www.coe.int/t/e/human_rights/esc/7_resources/Digest_en.pdf.
[6] ECSR, *Conclusions* XIII-2 (General Introduction), paras. 4 and 6–7.
[7] D. HARRIS and J. DARCY, *The European Social Charter*, New York, Transnational Publishers, 2001, 186.
[8] ECSR, *Conclusions* I; L. SAMUEL, *Fundamental Social Rights. Case Law of the European Social Charter*, Strasbourg, Council of Europe Publishing, 2002, 353.
[9] ECSR, *Conclusions* XIII-2 (General Introduction), para. 52.
[10] The Committee's perception of parental leave is that it "expresses a shift in the comparative importance of principles (the principle of equality between the sexes now takes precedence over the need to afford women specific protection, except in respect of maternity)." ECSR, *Conclusions* XIII-2 (General Introduction), para. 104.
[11] ECSR, *Conclusions* XIV-1, 364 (Greece); HARRIS and DARCY, supra note 9, 189.
[12] ECSR, *Conclusions* XIII-2 (General Introduction), para. 28; HARRIS and DARCY, supra note 9, 198.

Elements of the protection offered concern mainly social rights and material protection, such as family benefits and tax measures, i.e. *economic* protection.[13] However, attention is also paid to less or non-material issues, such as family counselling services, child care services, and work-family life.

Social protection requires a "combination of measures enabling the family to live together in society",[14] i.e. housing, family reunion, parental leave and social structures for assistance to families.[15] Social protection requires both social benefits and social services, such as family counselling services. The latter have been emphasized in particular with regard to reproductive health.[16] Gradually, more attention is being paid to family counselling services next to mediation services. Social services should not only be available, but also accessible, in particular in times of difficulty. In recent years, the ECSR has shown an increasing interest in family counselling and psychological guidance advice on child rearing.[17] Since at least 2004, is has started to ask for up-to-date information on the number of persons benefiting from the service, the number of staff involved,[18] coverage, accessibility and affordability.[19] However, the Committee does not seem to take any action upon the receipt of information: it simply takes note of the information provided by the state[20] or notes that the situation has not changed and was earlier considered to be in conformity.[21]

Legal protection of the family is assured through the legal status of children, equality between spouses, parental equality in the area of family responsibilities,[22] and equal parental rights within and outside marriage.[23]

In the context of custody and guardianship, Article 16 (R)ESC has also been understood to include the right of children to express opinions on matters concerning them.[24]

---

[13] ECSR, *Conclusions* XIII-2 (General Introduction), para. 113.
[14] Ibid., para. 63.
[15] Ibid., para. 64.
[16] Ibid., para. 108 and ECSR, *Conclusions* XIII-2, 150 (Iceland).
[17] ECSR, *Digest of the Case Law* 2006 (Article 16), www.coe.int/t/e/human_rights/esc/7_resources/Digest_en.pdf.
[18] See e.g. ECSR, *Conclusions* 2004, vol. 2 (Lithuania), 380.
[19] See e.g. ECSR, *Conclusions* 2004, vol. 2 (Romania), 486.
[20] See e.g. ECSR, *Conclusions* 2006, vol. 2 (Norway).
[21] See e.g. ECSR, *Conclusions* XVII-1, vol. 1 (Finland), 180.
[22] SAMUEL, supra note 10, 355.
[23] ECSR, *Conclusions* XIII-2 (General Introduction), paras. 11 and 13.
[24] ECSR, *Conclusions* XIII-2 (General Introduction), para. 23.

Article 17 RESC recognizes "the right of children and young persons to grow up in an environment which encourages the full development of their personality and of their physical and mental capacities".[25]

The Committee has also indicated with regard to children placed in institutions – and there is no reason to assume that the same right would not apply to all children – that they are entitled to the highest possible degree of satisfaction of their developing emotional needs and their physical well-being.[26]

Several issues are being addressed under Article 17 RESC by the Committee: first of all, those that have to do with the status of the child, such as the establishment of parentage,[27] the rights of children not born of or within the marriage,[28] and protection of orphans and homeless children.[29] The guiding principle on issues with regard to the status of the child has been full equality for all children before the law in every respect:[30] "As to the status of the child, the Committee has chiefly endeavoured to further the principle of equality."[31]

A second field that the ECSR has entered into is the protection of young persons in general, be it with regard to ill-treatment (sexual ill-treatment and corporal punishment), the placement of children in an institution or young offenders.[32] In the XIIIth reporting cycle, a general question was added under Article 17 ESC, regarding three priority aspects in the Committee's view of the protection of young persons: the protection against ill-treatment, access to court and protection of young offenders.[33]

Protection against ill-treatment is also covered by Article 7(10), which offers protection against physical and moral dangers, also within the framework of the family.[34] In the view of the ECtHR, children who suffer from ill-treatment by their parents which the authorities know or should have known about, are entitled to adequate protective measures.[35]

---

[25] Compare Article 6 CRC which guarantees a right to life, survival and development.
[26] ECSR, *Conclusions* XVII-2 (Belgium), 84.
[27] ECSR, *Conclusions* XIII-2 (General Introduction), paras. 33–35.
[28] ECSR, *Conclusions* XIII-2 (General Introduction), para. 36.
[29] Ibid., paras. 45–51.
[30] Ibid., para. 44.
[31] Ibid., para. 30.
[32] See *inter alia* ECSR, *Conclusions* I (General Observation), 77.
[33] ECSR, *Conclusions* XIII-2 (General Introduction), para. 59.
[34] ECSR, *Conclusions* XIII-2 (General Introduction), para. 53 and 58.
[35] ECtHR, *Z. and others v. United Kingdom*, judgment of 10 May 2001.

With regard to placement in an institution, the Committee has emphasized that in order to be considered adequate, institutions are to provide a life of human dignity for the children placed therein and are to provide conditions promoting their growth physically, mentally and socially. A unit in a child welfare institution should be of such size as to resemble a home environment.[36]

More recently, access of children to (mainly civil) courts, *inter alia* when there are family conflicts, has received growing attention.[37]

2. HUMAN RIGHTS OF PARENTS

Although there is an explicit recognition of the rights and duties of parents in Article 17(a) (R)ESC, what the rights and duties of parents imply exactly has not been specified.[38] Arguably, central to the human rights of parents are the right to private and family life, as guaranteed by Article 8 of the European Convention on Human Rights:

> 1. Everyone has the right to respect for his private and family life, his home and his correspondence.
> 2. There shall be no interference by a public authority with the exercise of this right except such as is in accordance with the law and is necessary in a democratic society in the interests of national security, public safety or the economic well-being of the country, for the prevention of disorder or crime, for the protection of health or morals, or for the protection of the rights and freedoms of others.

In the view of the ECtHR, "the exercise of parental rights constitutes a fundamental element of family life".[39] Article 8 ECHR thus recognizes and protects the rights of parents to exercise parental authority over their children. As a consequence, parents have the right to restrict a child's liberty:

> The care and upbringing of children normally and necessarily require that the parents or an only parent decide where the child must reside and also impose, or authorize others to impose, various restrictions on the child's liberty. Thus the children in a school or other educational or recreational institution must abide by certain rules

---

[36] ECSR, *Conclusions* XVII-2 (Belgium), 84.
[37] ECSR, *Conclusions* XIII-2 (General Introduction), para. 59; HARRIS and DARCY, supra note 9, 199.
[38] Compare the references to the rights and duties of parents in Articles 5 and 18 CRC in particular.
[39] ECtHR, *R v. the United Kingdom*, judgment of 8 July 1987, para. 64; confirmed in ECtHR, *Nielsen v. Denmark*, Judgment of 28 November 1988, para. 61.

which limit their freedom of movement and their liberty in other respects. Likewise a child may have to be hospitalised for medical treatment.[40]

Parental rights commonly include rights of tutorship, custody and access. Article 2, Protocol 1 to the ECHR also guarantees the rights of parents to ensure that education and teaching is in conformity with their own religious and philosophical convictions.[41]

Tensions between the fundamental rights of children and of their parent(s) may arise, in particular in the event of a family crisis. Family life of parents with children obviously does not cease owing to the separation or divorce of the parents.[42] In the case of marriage breakdown, parents are entitled to concrete and appropriate assistance by competent state agents within a specific legal framework suited to the needs of separated parents and their underage child, in order to allow a separated parent (in the case at hand a father was concerned) to effectively enforce his parental and access rights.[43] Similarly, the biological father is entitled to be involved in the adoption process of his child, when the birth of the child is not the result of casual sex but fruit of a deliberate decision taken in the context of a loving relationship. Therefore, from the moment of the child's birth there existed between the biological father and his daughter a bond amounting to family life.[44]

Another sensitive area is that of a child being taken into care by public authorities. The mutual enjoyment by parents and child of each other's company is considered to be a fundamental element of family life. As a consequence, interference with the enjoyment of each other's company, i.e. by placing a child into care, is an interference with family life, and needs therefore to be in accordance with the law, serve a legitimate aim, and be necessary in a democratic society (i.e. in accordance with a pressing social need and proportionate to the aim pursued).[45]

While there is a margin of appreciation left for the state, given the fact that national authorities have the benefit of direct contact with all the persons concerned,[46] the

---

[40] ECtHR, *Nielsen v. Denmark*, judgment of 28 November 1988, para. 61.
[41] ECtHR, *Kjeldsen, Busk Madsen and Pedersen v. Denmark*, judgment of 7 December 1976, paras. 51–52.
[42] C. Ovey and R.C.A. White, *The European Convention on Human Rights*, Oxford, Oxford University Press, 2002, 229; ECtHR, *Hoffmann v. Austria*, judgment of 23 June 1993.
[43] ECtHR, *Zawadka v. Poland*, judgment of 23 June 2005.
[44] Ovey and White, supra note 40 232–233; ECtHR, *Keegan v. Ireland*, judgment of 26 May 1994.
[45] ECtHR, *Johansen v. Norway*, judgment of 7 August 1996, § 52; ECtHR, *H.K. v. Finland*, judgment of 26 September 2006, para. 105.
[46] See ECtHR, *Olsson v. Sweden (no. 2)*, judgment of 27 November 1992, para. 90.

guiding principles constraining that margin of appreciation are the best interests of the child and reunion of the family as soon as circumstances permit.

In the case of placement of children in institutions, the ECSR has stressed that any restrictions or limitations of custodial rights of parents should be based on adequate and reasonable criteria laid down in legislation. They should not go beyond what is necessary for the protection and best interest of the child and the rehabilitation of the family.[47]

Stricter scrutiny is called for in respect of any *further* limitations to parents' right to family life, beyond assessing the need to take a child into public care, such as limitations on parental rights of access. In the view of the ECtHR, such further limitations entail the danger that the family relations between the parents and a young child are effectively curtailed as the possibilities of reunification will be progressively diminished and eventually destroyed if the biological parent and the child are not allowed to meet each other at all or only so rarely that no natural bonding between them is likely to occur.[48]

As regards the extreme step of severing all parental links with a child, the Court has taken the view that such a measure would cut a child from its roots and could only be justified in exceptional circumstances or by the overriding requirement of the child's best interests.[49] Much depends nevertheless on the nature of the parent-child relationship: the severance of links between a child and father, who had never had care and custody of the child, has been found to fall within the margin of appreciation of the courts which had made the assessment of the child's best interests.[50]

Parents also enjoy some procedural guarantees: the decision-making process involved in measures of interference must be fair and such as to afford due respect to the interests safeguarded by Article 8 ECHR.[51] Effective participation in the decision-making process presupposes that a parent be placed in a position where he or she may obtain access to information which is relied on by the authorities in taking measures of protective care or in taking decisions relevant to the care and custody of a child.[52] Also, when a parent is deprived of parental rights, he is to be

---

[47] ECSR, *Conclusions* XV-2 (General Introduction), 29.
[48] ECtHR, *K. and T. v. Finland*, 12 July 2001, paras. 155 and 179.
[49] ECtHR, *Johansen v. Norway*, judgment of 7 August 1996, para. 84, ECtHR, *Gnahoré v. France*, judgment of 19 September 2000, para. 59.
[50] See ECtHR, *Söderbäck v. Sweden*, judgment of 28 October 1998, paras. 31–34.
[51] ECtHR, *W. v. the United Kingdom*, judgment of 8 July 1987, paras. 62 and 64.
[52] ECtHR, *McMichael v. the United Kingdom*, judgment of 24 February 1995, para. 92.

involved in the decision-making process to an extent necessary to protect his interests.[53]

Several conflicts of rights may arise: the right to family life of one parent versus the other parent, the right to family life of the biological parents versus the foster parents or the right to family life of the parents versus the best interests of the child.

In principle, a fair balance has to be struck between the interests of the child remaining in care and those of the parents in being reunited with the child.[54] In carrying out this balancing exercise, the Court attaches particular importance to the best interests of the child. Ultimately, when there is a real conflict of rights of children and parents, the fundamental rights of children may trump or override those of the parents. This may be the case, e.g. if a child has been staying with foster parents for years. In the latter case, it may be in the interest of the child not to have its *de facto* family situation changed again. Priority will then be accorded to the interest of the child over the right to family life of the parents: after a considerable period of time has passed since the child was originally taken into public care, the interest of a child not to have his or her *de facto* family situation changed again may override the interests of the parents to have their family reunited.[55]

If allegations of abuse have been made by a child, following which the child has been taken into protective care, a parent may have an interest in being informed of the nature and extent of the allegations, as long as the disclosure of a child's statements do not place it at risk.[56]

An extreme example is a conflict between the right to family life of international adoptive parents who have not yet created a family tie, with the interests and views of the adoptive children. Priority has been given by the ECtHR to the interests of the children.[57]

---

[53] ECtHR, *Hunt v. Ukraine*, jugdment of 7 December 2006, para. 60.
[54] ECtHR, *Olsson v. Sweden (no. 2)*, judgment of 27 November 1992, para. 90, and ECtHR, *Hokkanen v. Finland*, judgment of 23 September 1994, para. 55.
[55] ECtHR, *K.A. v. Finland*, judgement of 14 January 2003, para. 138; ECtHR, *R. v. Finland*, judgment of 30 May 2006, para. 89.
[56] ECtHR, *T.P. and K.M. v United Kingdom*, judgment of 10 May 2001, para. 80.
[57] ECtHR, *Pini and Bertani and Manera and Atripaldi v. Romania*, judgment of 22 June 2004, paras. 155–166.

3. RESPONSIBILITIES OF PARENTS

Article 18 CRC mentions the principle that both parents have common responsibilities for the upbringing and development of the child. Parents or legal guardians are assigned the primary responsibility for the upbringing and development of the child. The best interests of the child are to be their basic concern. Inspiration for the determination of the responsibilities of parents could also be drawn from the aims of education, i.e. the development of the child's personality, talents and mental and physical abilities to their fullest potential, the development of respect for human rights, the development of respect for parents, own identity, national values and other civilizations, the preparation of the child for responsible life in a free society and the development of respect for the natural environment (Article 29 CRC). As the CRC Committee has explained in its first General Comment,

> These aims, set out in the five subparagraphs of article 29 (1) are all linked directly to the realization of the child's human dignity and rights, taking into account the child's special developmental needs and diverse evolving capacities. The aims are: the holistic development of the full potential of the child (29 (1) (a)), including development of respect for human rights (29 (1) (b)), an enhanced sense of identity and affiliation (29 (1) (c)), and his or her socialization and interaction with others (29 (1) (d)) and with the environment (29 (1) (e)).[58]

The (R)ESC does not contain a similarly worded, explicit description of the responsibilities of parents and caregivers. The responsibility of parents can however be deduced from the rights of children – as evoked in Article 17(1) RESC – to "an environment which encourages the full development of their personality and of their physical and mental capacities". It can also be assumed that parents, just like institutions, should aim at the "highest degree of satisfaction of their [children's] emotional needs and physical well-being."[59]

In the view of the ECtHR, parents have a natural duty towards their children for "education and teaching". In other words, their right to have their religious and philosophical convictions respected in education "corresponds to a responsibility closely linked to the enjoyment and the exercise of the right to education".[60]

---

[58] CRC Committee, General Comment No. 1 (2001), *The Aims of Education*, para. 1.
[59] ECSR, *Conclusions* XVII-2 (Belgium), p 84.
[60] ECtHR, *Kjeldsen, Busk Madsen and Pedersen v. Denmark*, judgment of 7 December 1976, para. 52; ECtHR, *Folgerø and others v. Norway*, judgment of 29 June 2007, para. 84.

4. OBLIGATIONS OF THE STATE

Many of the rights of children and parents are mirrored in corresponding obligations for the state. In a way, they are two sides of the same coin.

The (R)ESC imposes some clear obligations on State Parties. In line with Article 7(10), states are to take measures to protect children against dangers to which they may be exposed by their families or close surroundings.[61] Article 16 contains an obligation to implement a true family policy.[62] It is recognition of the fact that family welfare cannot be left to individual effort alone.[63] Article 17(1)(a) requires states to ensure that children and young persons have the care, the assistance, the education and the training they need. The obligation of the state is qualified, however, in that Article 17(1) explicitly provides that the rights and duties of parents are to be taken into account.

The division of responsibility and obligations between the state and society is that state action is not necessary to the extent that private sources provide sufficient protection. This follows from the wording that states agree to "take all appropriate and necessary" measures of protection.[64] These measures include the establishment or maintenance of appropriate institutions (such as children's homes and nurseries) or services (such as the provision of guidance and assistance).[65]

4.1. OBLIGATION TO PROTECT AGAINST CORPORAL PUNISHMENT

The ECtHR has held that a state is to be held responsible under Article 3 ECHR (prohibition of torture, inhuman or degrading treatment or punishment) for the beating of children by their parents or other individuals.[66] It argued:

> The Court considers that the obligation on the High Contracting Parties under Article 1 of the Convention to secure to everyone within their jurisdiction the rights and freedoms defined in the Convention, taken together with Article 3, requires States to take measures designed to ensure that individuals within their jurisdiction are not subjected to torture or inhuman or degrading treatment or punishment, including such ill-treatment administered by private individuals [...]. Children and other vulnerable individuals, in particular, are entitled to State protection, in the form of effective deterrence, against such serious breaches of personal integrity [...].

---

[61] SAMUEL, supra note 10, 376.
[62] ECSR, *Conclusions* I; SAMUEL, supra note 10, 353.
[63] ECSR, *Conclusions* I (General Observation), 75.
[64] ECSR, *Conclusions* 1 (Italy), 77.
[65] ECSR, *Conclusions* III, 80.
[66] ECtHR, *A v. United Kingdom*, judgement of 23 September 1998, para. 22.

Which acts or behaviour amount to a violation of Article 3 ECHR is less clear, although the Court tends to apply a stricter approach than before. Repeatedly beating a nine year old child with a garden cane, which is applied with considerable force, clearly does.[67] On the other hand, three "whacks" on the bottom of an eight year old boy through shorts with a rubber-soled gym shoe, with no one else but the headmaster administering the whacks present, were found not to amount to a degrading punishment.[68]

The ECSR has taken a more straightforward approach. It has qualified as contrary to Article 17 of the Charter every form of violence, ill-treatment or abuse, whether physical or mental. In its view, "there can[not] be any educational value in corporal punishment of children that cannot be otherwise achieved."[69]

It therefore expects states to prohibit *any* form of corporal punishment of children, as an important measure for the education of the population in that it gives a clear message about what society considers to be acceptable. This overall prohibition "avoids discussions and concerns as to where the borderline would be between what might be acceptable corporal punishment and what is not." In conclusion, the Committee considers that Article 17 requires a prohibition in legislation against any form of violence against children, whether at school, in other institutions, in their home or elsewhere. It furthermore considers that any other form of degrading punishment or treatment of children must be prohibited in legislation and combined with adequate sanctions in penal or civil law.[70] This position was repeated in the ECSR's findings in collective complaints of the World Organization against Torture against Greece, Ireland and Belgium. It held: "The Committee's case law is to the effect that the prohibition of all the forms of violence must have a legislative basis. The prohibition must cover all forms of violence regardless of where it occurs or of the identity of the alleged perpetrator. Furthermore the sanctions available must be adequate, dissuasive and proportionate."[71] In support of this position, the ECSR relies also on recommendations of the Council of Ministers and the Parliamentary Assembly of the Council of Europe.[72]

---

67 Ibid., para. 21.
68 ECtHR, *Costello-Roberts v. United Kingdom*, judgment of 25 March 1993, para. 32.
69 ECSR, *Conclusions* XV-2 (General Introduction), 29.
70 ECSR, *Conclusions* XV-2 (General Introduction), 29.
71 See, e.g. ECSR, Collective Complaint No. 17/2003, *World Organisation against Torture v. Greece*, para. 39.
72 PARLIAMENTARY ASSEMBLY, Recommendation 1666 (2004) "Europe-wide ban on corporal punishment of children", 24 June 2004; COMMITTEE OF MINISTERS, Recommendation No. R (93) 2 on the medico-social aspects of child abuse, 22 March 1993; COMMITTEE OF MINISTERS, Recommendation No. R (90) 2 on social measures concerning violence within the family, 15

The Belgian member of the Committee, François, has dissented in all three cases, arguing that:

> the Committee's extensive application of Article 17 of the Charter in connection with children's upbringing can be contested on two counts: intellectually, because it is excessive, and morally, because it is unjust. Excessive: it strikes me as disproportionate to use such magniloquent terms as "human dignity", "degrading treatment" and "physical integrity" to condemn conduct as innocent, in terms of intent and effect, as a slap on the hand or a smack on the bottom administered by a parent, in the child's interests, to a young child who will not listen to reason and persists with dangerous behaviour. Indeed, trivialising the important concept of human dignity through ill-considered use actually undermines human dignity.
> Unjust: it is time we remembered that the law is entitled to prohibit only actions that are harmful to society (1789 Declaration of the Rights of Man, Article 5). There is no scientific proof that the punishments I have just mentioned are harmful, or indeed useless as a means of bringing up a child. To condemn without reservation these measures seems to me to be based on ideological or aesthetic considerations than on rational argument.
> Admittedly, any educational choice may be re-examined, but I find it shocking to lump together categories of people as different as child abusers and parents who take care to use moderate correction towards their children.

In sum, the European Court of Human Rights requires a certain threshold of severity in order to qualify corporal punishment of children as a violation of Article 3 ECHR. The ECSR has qualified *any* form of violence against children as contrary to the Charter, and thus upholds a higher standard of protection. On the other hand, the ECSR mainly insists on a legal prohibition of violence against children, while the ECtHR has laid more emphasis on the effectiveness of protection offered.

4.2. OBLIGATION TO PROTECT CHILDREN AGAINST NEGLECT AND ABUSE

The state is under an obligation to take adequate and effective protective measures against neglect and abuse by parents. This includes reasonable steps to prevent ill-treatment of which the authorities had or ought to have had knowledge.[73] If a state fails to protect children from serious, long-term neglect and abuse, this amounts to a violation of Article 3 ECHR, which prohibits torture and inhuman or degrading treatment or punishment. A state is not only to abstain from these

---

January 1990; COMMITTEE OF MINISTERS, Recommendation No. R(85)4 on violence within the family, 26 March 1985.

[73] ECSR, *Conclusions* XV-2 (General Introduction).

acts itself, but it is also under an obligation to prevent individuals from committing the said acts.[74]

Obviously, difficult and sensitive decisions are to be made here. Moreover, there is an important countervailing obligation of respecting and preserving family life (cf. supra).

4.3. OBLIGATION TO RESPECT FAMILY LIFE

As to taking children into care, authorities enjoy a wide margin of appreciation in assessing the necessity of taking a child into care, in particular where an emergency situation arises. However, the state is to carry out a careful assessment of the impact of the proposed care measure on the parents and the child, as well as of the possible alternatives to taking the child into public care, prior to implementation of such a measure.[75]

The guiding principle for care orders is that they should be regarded as a temporary measure, to be discontinued as soon as circumstances permit, and that any measures implementing temporary care should be consistent with the ultimate aim of reuniting the natural parent and the child.[76] The aim of states' involvement in the upbringing and protection of children is therefore the rehabilitation of the biological family as far as possible, taking into consideration a child's interests.[77] The positive duty to take measures to facilitate family reunification as soon as reasonably feasible weighs on the competent authorities with progressively increasing force as from the commencement of the period of care, subject always to its being balanced against the duty to consider the best interests of the child.[78]

Moreover, procedural guarantees should be offered and in particular adequate involvement in the decision-making process concerning the care of one's child. Lack of such involvement amounts to a failure to respect family life and a breach of Article 8 of the ECHR.[79]

In case of further limitations beyond placement into care, the minimum to be expected of the authorities is to examine the situation anew from time to time to see whether there has been any improvement in the family's situation.[80]

---

74 ECtHR, *Z. and others v. United Kingdom*, judgment of 10 May 2001.
75 ECtHR, *K. and T. v. Finland*, judgment of 12 July 2001, para. 166, and ECtHR, *Kutzner v. Germany*, judgment of 26 February 2002, para. 67.
76 ECtHR, *Olsson v. Sweden (no. 1)*, judgment of 24 March 1988, para. 81.
77 SAMUEL, supra note 10, 376.
78 ECtHR, *K. and T. v. Finland*, judgment of 12 July 2001, para. 178.
79 ECtHR, *T.P. and K.M. v United Kingdom*, judgment of 10 May 2001, para. 83.
80 ECtHR, *K. and T. v. Finland* judgment of 12 July 2001, paras. 155 and 179.

Children taken into public care should as far as possible be placed within such a distance to their natural family that they can maintain links with it, unless considered undesirable for the child. Siblings should be kept together as far as possible.[81]

For the state, there is the challenge of properly balancing the obligation to protect children against abuse with the obligation to respect family life. If it intervenes too quickly, it may violate the right to family life. If it intervenes too late, it may be found to have failed in protecting against torture and inhuman or degrading treatment or punishment.[82]

4.4. OBLIGATION TO ASSIST IN ENFORCEMENT OF ACCESS ARRANGEMENTS

A state has also the obligation to assist a separated parent in the enforcement of access arrangements to his or her child. Some principles apply. First of all, the lack of cooperation between separated parents is not a circumstance which by itself exempts the authorities from their positive obligations. "It rather imposes on the authorities an obligation to take measures that would reconcile the conflicting interests of the parties, keeping in mind the paramount interests of the child."[83] Authorities should take practical steps that, "firstly, encourage the parties to co-operate in the enforcement of the access arrangements and, secondly, secure concrete and appropriate assistance by competent state agents within a specific legal framework suited to the needs of separated parents and their underage child." A failure in the positive obligation to provide a parent with assistance which would make it possible to effectively enforce parental and access rights, which leads to a complete loss of contact between the parent and the child, amounts to a violation of Article 8 ECHR.[84]

4.5. OBLIGATIONS RELATING TO PARTICULARLY VULNERABLE GROUPS OF CHILDREN

Special care and protection is to be granted to orphans and homeless children, so that their development and well-being are not too seriously impaired. For home-

---

[81] ECSR, *Conclusions* XV-2 (General Introduction). On the first point, see also COMMITTEE OF MINISTERS, Resolution (77)33 on placement of children, 3 November 1977 (point 2.11).
[82] See also M. VERHEYDE, "The Protection of Children's Rights by the European Court of Human Rights" in A. ALEN, H. BOSLY, M. DE BIE and others, *The UN Children's Rights Convention: Theory Meets Practice*, Antwerp, Intersentia, 110.
[83] ECtHR, *Zawadka v. Poland*, judgment of 23 June 2005, para. 67.
[84] Ibid.

less children, the nearest possible approximation to a home environment should be the overriding concern. Apart from the assurance of economic security, they are to be provided with care facilities suiting their needs in human terms.[85]

4.6. OBLIGATIONS RELATING TO EQUALITY

In the view of the ECSR, equality has been one of the main themes of its case law in relation both to the family's organization and to its protection, both within the parental couple and between all children regardless of their own or their parents' status.[86]

As to equality between children, full equality of all children before the law in every respect is to be guaranteed (status of the child, inheritance rights, etc.).[87]

4.7. OBLIGATIONS RELATED TO PROTECTION OF THE FAMILY

In order to allow for reconciliation of family and working life, the ECSR has paid attention to issues like parental leave[88] and child care services.[89]

More of interest for our assessment of an upbringing pledge in light of children's rights and human rights instruments within the Council of Europe is the attention the Committee has paid to family mediation services. In its 2006 reporting cycle, the Committee has focused in particular on family mediation services. Family mediation services help settle disputes and should ensure that future relations between parents and between them and their children are not unduly damaged. The Committee has scrutinized the conditions governing access (whether they are free of charge and whether they cover the whole country) as well as their effectiveness.[90]

The Committee has also paid attention to family assistance, such as parental education programmes,[91] and programmes and services designed to support parents

---

[85] ECSR, *Conclusions* XIII-2 (General Introduction), paras. 47–48.
[86] Ibid., para. 31.
[87] Ibid., para. 44.
[88] Ibid., para. 103.
[89] Ibid., para. 109.
[90] ECSR, *Conclusions* XVIII-1/2006 (General Introduction), para. 29. See also ECSR, *Conclusions* 2006, vol. 2 (Norway), 453–454.
[91] ECSR, *Conclusions* XV-1, vol. 2 (Norway), 453–454.

in their parental roles, such as programmes with an educational function, parents' and family counselling services and measures to provide parents with support.[92]

5. SOCIAL COHESION FRAMEWORK

The Council of Europe has been active in the field of family policy and social cohesion too.[93] In this field, it has been emphasized that parenting and the family cannot be left to family intimacy and the private sphere. In 2006, the Committee of Ministers submitted that "parenting, though linked to family intimacy, should be designated as a domain of public policy."[94] "While fully respecting the autonomy of the private sphere, the family is described as a fundamental unit in society with the right to appropriate social, legal and economic protection to ensure its full development."[95]

As a starting point, it is recognized that parents have the prime responsibility for their child,[96] except when the state has to intervene to protect the child.[97] Given this primary responsibility for parents, they are entitled to appropriate support from the state in fulfilling their parental functions.[98] This support should *inter alia* result from policies that support positive parenting.

Positive parenting is understood to mean "parental behaviour based on the best interests of the child that is nurturing, empowering, non-violent and provides recognition and guidance which involves setting of boundaries to enable the full development of the child".[99] Positive parenting is seen as a means of ensuring

---

[92] ECSR, *Conclusions* XV-1, vol. 1 (Greece), 306–310; ESCR, *Conclusions* XIV-1 (Austria), 89–92.
[93] For a general introduction, see e.g. *Social Cohesion Developments*, Special Issue No. 5 on Children and Families (May 2006), www.coe.int/t/dg3/socialpolicies/socialcohesiondev/source/Newsletter/Special-05-Family_en.pdf.
[94] COMMITTEE OF MINISTERS, Recommendation Rec(2006)19 of the to member states on policy to support positive parenting, 13 December 2006; Final Communiqué and Political Declaration of the European Ministers responsible for Family Affairs (28th session, May 2006).
[95] Explanatory report to Recommendation Rec(2006)19 of the Committee of Ministers to Member States on policy to support positive parenting, 13 December 2006, CM(2006)194 add, 27 November 2006.
[96] Appendix to Recommendation Rec(2006)19 of the Committee of Ministers to Member States on policy to support positive parenting, 13 December 2006.
[97] Explanatory report to Recommendation Rec(2006)19 of the Committee of Ministers to Member States on policy to support positive parenting, 13 December 2006, CM(2006)194 add, 27 November 2006.
[98] Ibid.
[99] Appendix to Recommendation Rec(2006)19 of the Committee of Ministers to Member States on policy to support positive parenting, 13 December 2006.

respect for and implementation of children's rights".[100] Positive parenting promotes the development of positive parent-child relationships and the optimization of the child's developmental potential.[101]

Policies supporting positive parenting require governments to "acknowledge the essential nature of families and of the parental role and [to] create the necessary conditions for positive parenting in the best interests of the child." [102] The qualitative aspects of parenting are to be supported.[103] Policies and measures in the field of support for parenting should not be paternalistic; rather, they should adopt a rights-based approach in which children and parents are treated as holders of rights and obligations.

6. CONCLUSION: AN UPBRINGING PLEDGE: OPTIONAL, RECOMMENDED OR MANDATORY?

Neither from a human rights perspective nor from a social cohesion framework has an upbringing pledge ever been mentioned as a necessary and mandatory tool for protection of the family and the observance of children's rights. Clearly, Articles 16 and 17 (R)ESC do not oblige states to create the institution of an upbringing pledge.

It seems equally difficult to maintain that children's rights as guaranteed in the (R)ESC, and as interpreted by the ECSR, lend support to the institution of an upbringing pledge. While the Committee has paid some attention to programmes and services aiming at supporting parents in their child rearing task, such as parent education and counselling, it has never expressed strong support, nor made any recommendations regarding these programmes and services. Moreover, attention paid to supporting policies for parents' child rearing capacities so far has always been from the perspective of the right of families to protection, not from that of the rights of children. Within a social cohesion framework, emphasis has been put on mutuality and partnership between parents and children.[104]

---

[100] COMMITTEE OF MINISTERS, Recommendation Rec(2006)19 of the to Member States on policy to support positive parenting, 13 December 2006.
[101] Explanatory report to Recommendation Rec(2006)19 of the Committee of Ministers to Member States on policy to support positive parenting, 13 December 2006, CM(2006)194 add, 27 November 2006.
[102] COMMITTEE OF MINISTERS, Recommendation Rec(2006)19 of the to Member States on policy to support positive parenting, 13 December 2006.
[103] Explanatory report to Recommendation Rec(2006)19 of the Committee of Ministers to Member States on policy to support positive parenting, 13 December 2006, CM(2006)194 add, 27 November 2006.
[104] COMMITTEE OF MINISTERS, Recommendation Rec(2006)19 of the to Member States on policy to support positive parenting, 13 December 2006 and appendix 1.

While mutuality and partnership presuppose *reciprocal* commitments, an upbringing pledge implies a commitment from only one side, i.e. the parent(s) or caregiver(s).

At the other end of the spectrum, an upbringing pledge does not seem to run counter to children's rights. Therefore, no objection from a children's rights' perspective can be raised against an upbringing pledge.

Given the increasing focus on child rearing failures of parents, and the creation of supportive policies, programmes and services in the field of child rearing, the ECSR will most likely receive more information on the issue in the near future. It may then also take a clearer stance on desirability and modalities of the said policies, programmes and services. It seems unlikely however that it would do so from the perspective of Article 17 (R)ESC, which offers legal, social and economic protection to children. Rather, the protection of the family as guaranteed in Article 16 is likely to be the prism through which these new developments are scrutinized.

From the perspective of a more effective implementation of children's rights, in particular the right "to grow up in an environment which encourages the full development of their personality and of their physical and mental capacities", the upbringing pledge may have little to offer, being a non-enforceable commitment. It may nevertheless have some educational and awareness raising value.

RECONCILING HUMAN RIGHTS OF WOMEN AND CHILDREN

Ineke Boerefijn[1]

"Compromising women's rights is not an option."[2]

1. INTRODUCTION

Children's rights are inextricably linked to women's rights. Advancing the position of women will positively influence the position of children – in terms of UNICEF this is the 'double dividend' of gender equality.

> Healthy, educated and empowered women are more likely to have healthy, educated and confident daughters and sons. Women's autonomy, defined as the ability to control their own lives and to participate in making decisions that affect them and their families, is associated with improved child nutrition (…). Other aspects of gender equality, such as education levels among women, also correlate with improved outcomes for children's survival and development.[3]

Ensuring women's rights requires a two-tier track. The elimination of discrimination against women, with specific attention to the eradication of poverty, the promotion of women's health and the prevention and combating of violence against women and girls requires priority attention from all actors. This will not only be beneficial immediately to women, but also to children. At the same time, a long-term perspective must be taken into account. Achieving genuine equality of women and men requires measures aimed at changing the traditional division of family responsibilities. This requires specific attention for the position of women

---

[1] Opzij Chair, Centre for Gender and Diversity, Maastricht University; Associate Professor, Netherlands Institute of Human Rights (SIM), Utrecht School of Law. The author thanks Marjolein van den Brink for her valuable comments to previous versions of this chapter and Esther van der Weele for her research assistance.

[2] Yakin Ertürk, Special Rapporteur on violence against women, in: UN Doc. A/HRC/4/34, *Report of the Special Rapporteur on violence against women, its causes and consequences, Yakin Ertürk. Intersections between culture and violence against women,* par. 71.

[3] UNICEF, *Women and children. The double dividend of equality. State of the world's children 2007.* New York: UNICEF, 2007, p. 2.

and girls in education, access to the labour market and public and political participation.

In discussions on the introduction of an upbringing pledge it must be taken into consideration that such an instrument may have a different impact on women than men. This contribution examines the position of women and mothers in society, to see which relevant differences exist and need to be taken into consideration. The point of departure is the obligation of States to guarantee human rights of women, mothers and girls, in the public as well as the private sphere. International human rights law imposes a series of obligations on States. Embedding an upbringing pledge in a policy aimed at the advancement of women's rights is a precondition for its acceptability.

The following sections deal with the position of women in the public sphere, in particular in the field of employment, public and political participation, and education. Subsequently, attention is paid to the position of women in the family, paying specific attention to equal rights to enter into marriage, during marriage and at its dissolution, sexual and reproductive rights and the right to be free from violence. These sections are largely based on the Convention on the Elimination of Discrimination Against Women (hereafter: Women's Convention) and the interpretation thereof by the Committee on the Elimination of Discrimination Against Women (hereafter: CEDAW). The final section examines how the advancement of women's rights and children's rights can be reconciled. First, a brief overview of the importance of equal rights of women and men is presented.

2. EQUALITY OF THE SEXES

Worldwide structural discrimination against women has led to inequality in many fields, such as health, housing, work, education and within the family. Everywhere women and girls are victims of violence in the public and the private sphere on a large scale. The Convention on the Elimination of all forms of Discrimination Against Women contains different types of obligations for States. First, it is crucial that the law guarantees equality of women and men and prohibits discrimination (see especially Article 2(a) and (b) of the Women's Convention). While in many states discriminatory legislative provisions have been eliminated, in other states discriminatory laws continue to exist. For example, laws that give fathers more authority over there children than mothers, can be considered discriminatory and criminal codes that do not protect women against marital rape do not provide adequate protection against violations of their physical integrity. The Women's Convention obliges State Parties to ensure that laws that are on their face neutral do not discriminate against women in effect. For example, laws that distinguish between full-time and part-time employees may have a discriminatory effect on women, since women more often have part-time jobs than men.

Obviously, equality in and before the law is not sufficient. The Women's Convention not only requires State Parties to ensure *de jure* equality of women and men, but also to guarantee equality in practice. Where appropriate, they should take temporary special measures to achieve equality (see Article 4 of the Convention). The Committee on the Elimination of Discrimination Against Women (CEDAW), the organ established under the Women's Convention to monitor its implementation, has repeatedly recommended that State Parties take measures to increase the number of women in political and public organs, so as to accelerate their equal participation in decision-making.[4] The Women's Convention contains unique obligations in Articles 2(f) and 5, obliging State Parties to address the root causes of discrimination against women. Discrimination is often caused by traditional and religious customs, reflecting and upholding stereotyped views of the roles of women and men in society. Article 2(f) of the Convention requires States to 'modify or abolish existing laws, regulations, customs and practices which constitute discrimination against women', and Article 5(a) obliges State Parties 'to modify the social and cultural patterns of conduct of men and women, with a view to achieving the elimination of prejudices and customary and all other practices which are based on the idea of the inferiority or the superiority of either of the sexes or on stereotyped roles for men and women.' These provisions entail far-reaching obligations for State Parties. They are not only required to apply these provisions in relation to each of the substantive provisions of the Convention, but also as an autonomous obligation. States must also eliminate customs and traditions that have a negative impact on the position of women in areas that are not covered by the Convention. In its work the CEDAW has stressed that traditional and religious customs cannot justify the perpetuation of discrimination against women. The Convention thus seeks to end the perception that women are primarily (potential) mothers, while at the same time recognizing women's important reproductive functions. It is based on the idea that parenthood entails responsibilities for women and men and society as a whole.[5]

Various factors contribute to the present day reality, in which women provide for the care and rearing of children to a significantly larger extent than men. Further, it must be realized that single parent households are mostly female headed households. Also other carers are often women, such as neighbours and grandmothers helping out. Even where equal legal responsibilities have been defined,

---

[4] See Article 4 of the Women's Convention and CEDAW, General Recommendation No. 25, *Temporary special measures*, in: UN Doc. A/59/38 Part I, Annex I.

[5] W.C. Monster, E. Cremers and L. Willems, *Vrouwenverdrag, moederschap, ouderschap en arbeid* [The Women's Convention, motherhood, parenthood and employment]. Den Haag: Ministerie van Sociale Zaken, 1996, p. 50.

equal sharing responsibilities rarely exist in practice. As a result, the consequences of the introduction of an upbringing pledge would be much larger for women than men. One of the suggested formulations of the upbringing pledge is *'We* will be there for you',[6] but this could result in women feeling even more responsible for compensating the smaller part that men undertake in child rearing. If an upbringing pledge is indeed introduced, the fundamental differences between the position of women and men, both in society and within the family, should be taken into account. Otherwise the upbringing pledge will contribute to maintaining and possibly even reinforcing the inequality of women and men.

The importance of ending discrimination against women has been recognized since the establishment of the United Nations. It has been formulated as one of the main goals of the United Nations as demonstrated by the prominent place of the principle of equality in the UN Charter,[7] the Millennium Development Goals,[8] and the numerous declarations and treaties aimed at the elimination of discrimination against women. Putting an end to discrimination is not only beneficial to the enjoyment of human rights by women, it will advance society as a whole. In terms of the preamble of the Women's Convention, discrimination of women 'hampers the growth of the prosperity of society and the family.' The Beijing Declaration, adopted as the final outcome document of the Fourth World Conference on Women, provides that 'women's empowerment and their full participation on the basis of equality in all spheres of society, including participation in the decision-making process and access to power, are fundamental for the achievement of equality, development and peace.'[9]

---

[6] 'Belofte maakt schuld. De opvoedingsbelofte als kader voor de ouder-kindrelatie', [Promise is debt. The upbringing pledge as a framework for the parent-child relationship.] In: Hoger Instituut voor Gezinswetenschappen *et al., Van huwelijkscontract naar opvoedingsbelofte*, Brussel: Hoger Instituut voor Gezinswetenschappen, 2006, p. 9 (emphasis added, IB).

[7] Article 1 of the UN Charter states: 'The purposes of the United Nations are … 3. To achieve international co-operation in solving international problems of an economic, social, cultural or humanitarian character, and in promoting and encouraging respect for human rights and for fundamental freedoms for all without distinction as to race, sex, language or religion.'.

[8] Millennium Development Goal No. 3: Promote gender equality and empower women. The Millennium Development Goals are drawn from the Millennium Declaration, A/RES/55/2, adopted on 8 September 2000.

[9] UN Doc. A/CONF.177/20, *Report of the Fourth World Conference on Women, Annex I, Beijing Declaration*, par. 13.

3. THE POSITION OF WOMEN IN THE PUBLIC SPHERE

3.1. EMPLOYMENT AND ECONOMIC INDEPENDENCE OF WOMEN

The right to work is a fundamental right of all women, giving them the opportunity to provide for themselves. As guaranteed in Article 11 of the Women's Convention, all women, including women with children, and women with and without partners, have the right of access to the labour market. States are obliged to take measures to guarantee women's right to work and to increase women's participation at the labour market. Economic independence strengthens women's position in the family and in society. Employment outside the house enhances the possibilities to participate in public and political decision-making; it broadens and strengthens women's personal networks, and makes their position in the family stronger. Women who have no income of their own have a lower status in the family, and have less control over decisions relating to matters such as family expenditure and choice of residence.

The situation in the Netherlands may serve as an illustration. No more than approximately 40% of all women are economically independent. This implies that 60% of all Dutch women are financially dependent on their partner or on social benefits from the State. The Dutch government considers a person to be economically independent if she or he earns 70% of the legally established minimum wage. Between 2000 and 2004 the percentage of economically independent women aged 15–64 rose from 39% to 42%. This rise occurred in 2001 only, since then it remained unchanged. Also among men the percentage of economically independent rose in 2001; however, it subsequently decreased from 72% in 2001 to 69% in 2004. The percentage of economically independent women is lowest in families with three or more children (36%); the percentage of economically independent men in such families is 88%. In families without children, only 46% of women are economically independent, compared to 73% of men.[10] Further, the gender pay gap continues to exist, and women are underrepresented in higher positions at work.[11]

The 2007 ILO global report on equality at work shows that at the global level the position of women in employment has improved somewhat. Yet, the labour force participation rates of women and men continue to differ. In 2004 53% of

---

[10] Wil Portegijs (SCP), Brigitte Hermans (CBS), Vinodh Lalta (CBS), *Emancipatiemonitor 2006. Veranderingen in de leefsituatie en levensloop*, [Emancipation Monitor 2006. Changes in living conditions and course of life.] Den Haag: Sociaal en Cultureel Planbureau / Centraal Bureau voor de Statistiek, 2006, p. 192–194; Figuur 7.5 & Tabel 7.8.

[11] Emancipatiemonitor 2006, supra note 10, p. 181–185.

women were employed, as compared to 77.5% of men. Women find themselves more often in unpaid jobs, lower paid jobs, jobs in the informal sector or in lower-quality jobs in self-employment. The ILO report reveals that the gender pay gap and the underrepresentation of women remain a cause of concern, especially bearing in mind the Millennium Development Goals.[12]

Women's labour force participation is hindered by, among others, the lack of high quality and affordable child care facilities. As a consequence, women often resort to part-time functions when children are born where the family income so permits. The income rendered by part-time functions is often insufficient to consider them to be economically independent. A significant portion of women leaves the labour force entirely, either temporarily or not, because combining work and family responsibilities is stressful and difficult. In the Netherlands, in 2004, the income of women with three or more children was 37% of men in this group.[13] People who wish to combine family responsibilities with employment meet with various practical obstacles, because the organization of society is based on the availability of one parent to look after children outside school hours. Where women cannot afford to work part-time instead of full-time, they are as a consequence left with the double burden of working and having the lion's share of family responsibilities. The situation is particularly precarious for single parents – generally single mothers.

3.2. PARTICIPATION IN PUBLIC AND POLITICAL LIFE

The public and private spheres are still largely separate spheres. Traditionally women have participated in the public sphere to a lesser extent than men. This is particularly visible in women's underrepresentation in public bodies and political organs. Statistics from the Inter-Parliamentary Union show that the world average for women in parliaments is 17.4%, with figures varying per region, though in no region do women hold a majority in parliament.[14] As a consequence of their underrepresentation women are less involved in the development of public policy and in taking decisions that affect the organization of society and their private lives. Among the obstacles to women's participation in public and political life is their low rate of participation in the labour force, which is where candidates for positions in politics are often recruited from. Important political decisions are generally taken by those who hold powerful positions; participation in public and

---

[12] International Labour Organization, *Equality at work: Tackling the challenge, Global Report under the follow-up to the ILO Declaration on Fundamental Principles and Rights at Work.* Geneva: International Labour Office, 2007, p. 16–23.
[13] Emancipatiemonitor 2006, supra note 10, p. 185–186 and Figure 7.3.
[14] http://www.ipu.org/wmn-e/world.htm, last visited 7 October 2007.

political life is easier for people who are economically independent. According to the CEDAW:

> Women's economic dependence on men often prevents them from making important political decisions and from participating actively in public life. Their double burden of work and their economic dependence, coupled with the long or inflexible hours of both public and political work, prevent women from being more active. Stereotyping, including that perpetrated by the media, confines women in political life to issues such as the environment, children and health, and excludes them from responsibility for finance, budgetary control and conflict resolution. The low involvement of women in the professions from which politicians are recruited can create another obstacle.[15]

Since women are affected by political decisions it is crucial that they are involved in all matters, especially those that concern themselves and their children. Equal representation of women in politics and public organs will result in society that facilitates the combination of employment and family responsibilities – by both parents. Under Article 7 of the Women's Convention, that guarantees women's right to access to public and political bodies, State Parties must take measures to increase women's participation, if necessary by means of temporary special measures. After all, 'the just and effective organization of society demands the inclusion and participation of all its members.'[16]

3.3. EDUCATION

The importance of education for girls and women was recognized in the United Nations Millennium Development Goals, which include the elimination of gender disparity in primary and secondary education preferably by 2005, and at all levels by 2015. The gap between girls and boys enrolling in primary and secondary education is closing, but the adult literacy rate of women is 74%, of men 86% and most out of school children are girls.[17] The right to education is crucial for strengthening women's position in the labour market and in public and political positions. Educated women not only have better opportunities for employment and public participation, they are also less at risk of bearing children at a very young age, and bear fewer children. The CEDAW has labelled Article 10 of the Women's Convention as a key to women's development; it is the basic tool for women's empowerment in all spheres: in the workplace, in the family and in soci-

---

[15] CEDAW, General Recommendation No. 23, *Political and public life*, in: UN Doc. HRI/GEN/1/Rev.8, Compilation of general comments and general recommendations adopted by human rights treaty bodies, p. 318–329, par. 11–12.
[16] CEDAW, General Recommendation No. 23, supra note 15, par. 13.
[17] UNICEF, *State of the world's children*, supra note 3, Table 5.

ety. The low level of education of women and girls remains one of the most serious impediments to their full enjoyment of human rights. Under Article 10, State Parties are required to take all appropriate measures to eliminate discrimination against women in education at all levels, from pre-school to vocational training. The CEDAW encourages State Parties to prevent girls from dropping out of school, to receive education until a later age and to encourage them to enrol in education that is not traditionally 'female', such as technical education. Article 10 of the Women's Convention obliges State Parties to eliminate 'any stereotyped concept of the roles of men and women at all levels and in all forms of education by encouraging coeducation and other types of education which will help to achieve this aim and, in particular, by the revision of textbooks and school programmes and the adaptation of teaching methods.'

3.4. THE UPBRINGING PLEDGE AND EQUALITY OF WOMEN AND MEN IN THE PUBLIC SPHERE

While States have agreed that 'maternity, motherhood, parenting and the role of women in procreation must not be a basis for discrimination nor restrict the full participation of women in society,'[18] in practice this has not been achieved. The Women's Convention and CEDAW stress that full-time caring for children, and unequal sharing of family responsibilities between women and men are detrimental to women's position in society and in the family. Traditional views of the roles of women and men in public and private life result in inequalities in sharing family responsibilities and labour force participation. States are obliged to eliminate such stereotypes and to end discrimination in all fields of public life and to guarantee equal treatment of women and men not only in law, but also in practice. Motherhood should not constitute an obstacle to women's economic independence and to equal representation in public and political organs.

An upbringing pledge should not hinder the advancement of women and the improvement of their position in society. At present, women's share in child rearing is much larger than men's. The upbringing pledge should not become an instrument to hold women primarily responsible for caring for children and thus constitute an obstacle for the realization of their own human rights. The State must pursue a policy aimed at achieving equal responsibilities for child rearing. The stereotyped idea that working mothers are bad mothers must be eliminated. Mothers – and fathers – who combine employment and family responsibilities can be excellent parents. Furthermore, it is in the child's best interest to receive care from others rather than one parent, as this increases transparency and facil-

---

[18] UN Doc. A/CONF.177/20, supra note 9, Annex II, Platform for Action, par. 29.

itates early intervention in situations where the child is at risk of neglect or abuse.

Discussions on the upbringing pledge should take present day realities into account and should address the need to change these in the interests of children, women, men and society as a whole. If the introduction of an upbringing pledge is considered, international human rights law requires at least the following:

- Stress that child rearing is the joint responsibility of both parents.[19]
- Promote and facilitate access to employment and public and political bodies for both parents.
- Promote girls' education aimed at access to employment and also in non-traditional fields.
- Facilitate sharing of family responsibilities by both parents.
- Conduct awareness raising campaigns to eliminate stereotyped views of the roles of women as primarily responsible for child rearing and of men as primarily responsible for the family income.
- Take measures to facilitate the combination of employment and family responsibilities for single parents.

4. THE POSITION OF WOMEN IN THE FAMILY

4.1. INTRODUCTION

As mentioned in the previous section, child rearing responsibilities are not divided equally among partners. Many men are not willing to accept an equal share of family responsibilities, as they do not wish to interrupt their careers, consider child rearing not really interesting or consider this to be a woman's job. Also, many women consider themselves to be better equipped than men to look after children, and find it problematic to give up part of the responsibilities. The social environment may add to the pressure. In the Netherlands, a full-time working mother is called on by relatives and friends to explain her choice; a full-time working father is rarely questioned about his motivations. On the contrary, men who seek to diminish their working hours often encounter obstacles from their employers.

The sharing of family responsibilities is primarily a private matter; ideally, partners make their own decisions. Nevertheless, the State plays a crucial role in guaranteeing equality of women and men, also in the private sphere, in the relationship of spouses and in the relationship of parents and children. Article 16 of

---

[19] The term 'parents' includes also persons who carry out child rearing responsibilities without biological ties with the child.

the Women's Convention concerns the equality of women and men in the family and is one of the core provisions of the Convention. The CEDAW considers this provision so crucial that it has stated that reservations pertaining to Article 16 are not permitted as these are contrary to the object and purpose of the Convention.[20] Article 16 is one of the most detailed treaty provisions, identifying various areas in which discrimination against women continues to exist, which is further elaborated in a general recommendation of the CEDAW on this provision.[21] Discrimination in the private sphere is an obstacle to an equal position of both parents in respect of their children. The introduction of an upbringing pledge therefore requires equality also in the private sphere. The following sections deal with a selection of issues under Article 16 of the Women's Convention relevant to an equal position in the family.

4.2. EQUAL RIGHT TO ENTER INTO MARRIAGE, EQUAL RIGHTS DURING MARRIAGE AND AT ITS DISSOLUTION

Article 16 guarantees equal rights of women and men to enter into marriage. This may appear to be not a major problem in western societies; nevertheless, it is necessary to remain alert and to continue to prevent forced marriages and to remove obstacles to marrying the partner of one's choice if he or she is not a citizen of the country. Arranged marriages are not *per se* in violation of women's rights, but the arrangements should not in fact be a forced marriage. The CEDAW has stated that polygamous marriages violate Article 16 of the Women's Convention. It has stated that such marriages 'can have such serious emotional and financial consequences for her and her dependants that such marriages ought to be discouraged and prohibited.'[22] Practices such as *levirate*, the custom according to which a woman marries one of her husband's brothers after her husband's death, are in violation of Article 16.[23] The betrothal of girls or undertakings by family members on their behalf contravenes a woman's right freely to choose her partner.[24] Relationships

---

[20] CEDAW, 'Statements on reservations to the Convention on the Elimination of All Forms of Discrimination against Women', in: A/53/38/Rev.1, *Report of the Committee on the Elimination of Discrimination against Women, eighteenth and nineteenth sessions, General Assembly Official Records, Fifty-third session, Supplement No. 38*, New York: United Nations, 1998, Part Two, Chapter I.A, par. 8.

[21] CEDAW, General Recommendation No. 21, 'Equality in marriage and family relations', in: UN Doc. HRI/GEN/1/Rev.8, *Compilation of general comments and general recommendations adopted by human rights treaty bodies*, p. 308–317.

[22] CEDAW, General Recommendation No. 21, supra note 21, par. 14.

[23] CEDAW, Concluding observations on Togo, in: CEDAW/C/TGO/CO/5, par. 13–14.

[24] CEDAW, General Recommendation No. 21, supra note 21, par. 38.

that are not based on the free and full consent of both partners cannot be a fruitful basis for an equal relationship.

The CEDAW has stressed that the marriageable age of women and men must be 18, in accordance with the Convention on the Rights of the Child. Early marriage of girls often leads to dropping out from school and restricts their possibilities for economic independence. The CEDAW has pointed out that this not only affects women personally but also limits the development of their skills and independence and reduces access to employment, thereby detrimentally affecting their families and communities.[25] Early marriage can lead to early pregnancies that are detrimental to girls' health. The CEDAW considers the prohibition of betrothal and marriage of children (Article 16(2)) an important factor in preventing the physical and emotional harm which arise from early childbirth.[26]

Women and men have the same rights during marriage. Even in societies where men are no longer considered to be the head of the family under the law,[27] in practice they often act as such either for traditional reasons, imitating the customs of parents or because they are the breadwinner. This implies that in many families, men decide on important family issues such as finances and residence. The CEDAW stresses the importance of equal family responsibilities of partners. It states that:

> 'The shared rights and responsibilities enunciated in the Convention should be enforced at law and as appropriate through legal concepts of guardianship, wardship, trusteeship and adoption. States parties should ensure that by their laws both parents, regardless of their marital status and whether they live with their children or not, share equal rights and responsibilities for their children.'[28]

Legislation, i.e. often customary laws and customary practices, often affect women's status in marriage. For example, adultery by a married woman may constitute a ground for divorce for her husband, but not *vice versa*. Women who do not have the right to terminate a marriage, because the law does not provide for divorce, may be forced to stay in a marriage. Where divorce is legally possible, this may have unacceptable financial consequences for women. Many women are economically dependent on their male partners, because the responsibility for child rearing interrupts their own careers. A divorce can make women's lives much more difficult and can result in poverty for themselves and their children. An upbringing pledge should not have as a consequence that women are discouraged from seeking a divorce.

---

25 CEDAW, General Recommendation No. 21, supra note 21, par. 37.
26 CEDAW, General Recommendation No. 24, Article 12: Women and health, in: HRI/GEN/1/Rev.8, *Compilation of general comments and general recommendations adopted by human rights treaty bodies*, p. 329–339, par. 28.
27 Until 1971 the Dutch Civil Code provided that men were the head of the marital union.
28 CEDAW, General Recommendation No. 21, supra note 21, par. 20.

Divorce generally changes the sharing of family responsibilities, often to the effect that one of the former partners, generally the woman, carries out a much larger share of the responsibilities than the other former partner. It is necessary that both partners comply with their responsibilities; also the former husband should continue to be involved in child rearing, provided that this does not conflict with women's rights. It must be ensured that a perpetrator of domestic violence cannot invoke an upbringing pledge to demand and obtain access to a shelter where a battered woman resides with her children.

States are under an obligation to guarantee equality before the law, and must therefore also ensure that customary laws and practices do not violate the Women's Convention. Even though this may not be easy to achieve, equality in the family is of crucial importance and constitutes a precondition for equality in society.

4.3. SEXUAL AND REPRODUCTIVE RIGHTS

At present, every minute a woman dies in childbirth, especially in developing countries.[29] The Millennium Development Goals call for a 75% reduction in maternal mortality by 2015. The three pronged strategy to accomplish this goal contains the following elements: access to contraception to avoid unintended pregnancies, access to skilled care at the time of birth and timely access to quality emergency obstetric care in case of complications. Clearly, pregnancies and childbirth can have a tremendous impact on the lives and health of women. And, as mentioned before, having children affects women's participation in society to a large extent. The enjoyment of their sexual and reproductive rights is therefore essential.

According to Article 16(1)(e) of the Women's Convention, women have the same right to determine freely and responsibly the number and spacing of their children. The CEDAW has interpreted this to mean that, in the end, women should have the right to decide on the number and spacing of children:

> The responsibilities that women have to bear and raise children affect their right of access to education, employment and other activities related to their personal development. They also impose inequitable burdens of work on women. The number and spacing of their children have a similar impact on women's lives and also affect their

---

[29] Information from http://www.unfpa.org/mothers/index.htm (last visited 10 October 2007). On the human rights dimension of maternal mortality see UN Doc. A/61/338, *Report of the Special Rapporteur on the right of everyone to the enjoyment of the highest attainable standard of physical and mental health.*

physical and mental health, as well as that of their children. For these reasons, women are entitled to decide on the number and spacing of their children.[30]

Both women and men have the right to access to the information, education and means to enable them to exercise the right to determine freely the number and spacing of children. According to the CEDAW, Article 16(1)(e), read in conjunction with Article 10(h), guarantees that neither the State, nor the woman's partner, may restrict her freedom to decide.[31] Legal requirements such as the consent of the husband to obtain contraceptives or sterilization, or having a certain number of children before sterilization may be carried out, constitute a violation of the Women's Convention.[32] Also, forced sterilizations constitute a violation of the Women's Convention. In a case against Hungary, the CEDAW dealt with the issue of a Roma woman who had been brought to hospital with complications at childbirth. In a situation of physical pain and emotional distress the woman was asked to sign an illegible note, which turned out to be a consent form for sterilization. Against her wishes, she was sterilized. The CEDAW concluded that Articles 10(h), 12 and 16(1)(e) of the Women's Convention had been violated, because Hungary had failed to provide her appropriate information and advice on family planning and had not ensured that the woman concerned gave her fully informed consent to be sterilized. As a consequence, the woman concerned was permanently deprived of her natural reproductive capacity.[33] Forced sex, sterilization, forced sterilization and forced termination of pregnancy constitute a violation of women's fundamental rights. If committed under specific circumstances, such violations can even constitute a war crime or a crime against humanity.[34]

The Women's Convention contains several provisions guaranteeing the right to information on birth control. Article 10(h) states in quite broad terms that State Parties must ensure access to 'specific educational information to help to ensure the health and well-being of families, including information and advice on family planning,' which is much more than providing information on birth control. In its concluding comments on Chile, the CEDAW recommended not only 'to strengthen measures aimed at the prevention of unwanted pregnancies among adolescents,' but specified that these measures should include, *inter alia*, 'educational measures for girls and boys aimed at responsible partnerships and parenthood.'[35] Article 24(2)(f) of the Convention on the Rights of the Child simi-

---

[30] CEDAW, General Recommendation No. 21, supra note 21, par. 21.
[31] CEDAW, General Recommendation No. 21, supra note 21, par. 22.
[32] See for example CEDAW, Concluding comments on Chile, in: UN Doc. A/54/38, *Report of the Committee on the Elimination of Discrimination Against Women*, par. 229.
[33] CEDAW, Communication No. 4/2000, *Szijjarto v. Hungary*, views of 14 August 2006, in UN Doc. CEDAW/C/36/D/4/2004.
[34] Articles 7 and 8 of the Rome Statute of the International Criminal Court.
[35] UN Doc. CEDAW/C/CHI/CO/4, Concluding comments on Chile, par. 18.

larly deals with access to family planning education and services, adding that States must develop programmes to guide parents.

Information and education about responsible parenthood to both girls and boys, women and men, should accompany information on birth control and pregnancy. In so doing, it is worthwhile addressing the elimination of prejudice. Stereotyped attitudes of the roles of women and men generally begin in the family where children are taught implicitly and explicitly how girls and boys and women and men ought to behave. Parents and future parents could be informed of their possible contributions to the eradication of stereotypes. Education can also play a role in this. Article 29(1)(d) of the Convention on the Rights of the Child obliges State Parties to guarantee that education is directed to the preparation of the child for responsible life in free society, in the spirit of among others, equality of the sexes.

4.4. VIOLENCE AGAINST WOMEN

Intimate partner violence is the most common form of violence experienced by women worldwide. Such violence includes a range of sexually, physically and psychologically coercive acts against women.[36] It is a manifestation of unequal power relations between women and men and reinforces this inequality. Gender-based violence constitutes a serious violation of women's human rights. Under international human rights law, including the Women's Convention, States are under an obligation to prevent and combat all forms of violence against women, and to ensure that tradition, custom and religion are not used to justify any form of violence. Various human rights are at stake, including the right to life, the right to freedom from torture and other cruel, inhuman or degrading treatment or punishment, the right to health and the right to non-discrimination and equality.[37]

Domestic violence against women harms children as well. Numerous children witness domestic violence, and studies reveal that 'the exposure of children to violence in their homes on a frequent basis, usually through fights between parents or between a mother and her partner, can severely affect a child's well-being, personal development and social interaction in childhood and adulthood.'[38] Further, intimate partner violence increases the risk of violence against children.[39] Women who wish to escape violence temporarily or wish to end the relationship

---

[36] UN Doc. A/61/122/Add.1, *In-depth study on all forms of violence against women. Report of the Secretary-General*, par. 112–113.

[37] UN Doc. A/RES/48/104, *Declaration on the Elimination of Violence Against Women*, 20 December 1993, article 3.

[38] UN Doc. A/61/299, *Rights of the child. Report of the independent expert for the United Nations study on violence against children*, par. 47, with further references.

[39] Idem.

with a violent partner permanently should not meet with obstacles, but should be assisted and supported. The failure of the State to act with due diligence to prevent and combat violence against women, also in the private sphere, constitutes a violation of human rights. It goes without saying that the rights and interests of the child are of paramount importance. However, a woman may never be subjected to any coercion to remain in a violent situation or to maintain contacts with a violent (ex-) partner 'for the children's sake.' This would violate her fundamental rights, including the right to security. Further, it conflicts with Article 19(1) of the Convention on the Rights of the Child, that obliges State Parties to protect children from all forms of physical or mental violence. Victims of violence have a right to protection, which concerns the women who suffer from domestic violence, as well as others who suffer from it as well.

4.5. AN UPBRINGING PLEDGE AND WOMEN'S RIGHT TO EQUALITY IN THE FAMILY

Equality in the family is far from a reality for many women. The root causes are the same as those described in the previous section. The subordination of women in the family and in society is upheld in the name of culture, and common strategies must be developed to resist oppressive practices, and to promote and uphold universal human rights while rejecting encroachments grounded in ethnocentric thinking.[40] As the Special rapporteur on violence against women rightly states: 'Compromising women's rights is not an option.'[41]

Discussions on the desirability of an upbringing pledge should take the current situation into account and ensure that such a measure does not have as an effect the strengthening of the *status quo* or even make women's position weaker. Instead, it should be examined if and to what extent the pledge could be used as a tool to combat existing discrimination. The following requirements flow from the present section:

- Take all appropriate measures to prevent forced marriages.
- Take all appropriate measures to prevent early marriages and pregnancies.
- Provide information on family planning to women and men, and girls and boys.
- Provide information on the consequences of pregnancies and the ensuing responsibilities and obligations for both parents.

---

[40] UN Doc. A/HRC/4/34, *Report of the Special Rapporteur on violence against women, supra* note 2 par. 70.
[41] UN Doc. A/HRC/4/34, *Report of the Special Rapporteur on violence against women, supra* note 2 par. 71.

- Guarantee that neither partners nor the State can restrict a woman's right to decide on the number and spacing of children.
- Take measures to strengthen women's position in the family.
- Take measures to eradicate stereotyped views of the role of women and men in the family.
- Take measures to ensure that both parents continue to fulfil their parental responsibilities upon divorce, provided that this does not violate women's human rights.
- Take all measures to prevent and combat violence against women.
- If an upbringing pledge is introduced, use it as an instrument to eradicate stereotypes and prejudices.

5. TOWARDS A HUMAN RIGHTS APPROACH

Some people consider the Convention on the Rights of the Child to be an instrument that stereotypes women as mothers and restricts their choices in life. Women must be available at all times to serve their children. In case of conflicting interests, the interest of the child prevails. Others consider the Women's Convention to be an instrument that wants women to be egocentric human beings, with children's interests subordinated to their right to lead a meaningful life.

However, a more constructive approach is to regard the two human rights instruments not as clashing, but as compatible and mutually reinforcing. Discussions on an upbringing pledge should be conducted on the basis of a human rights-based approach. Various provisions in the Women's Convention are directly beneficial to children, such as those on equal treatment, protection of motherhood and shared family responsibilities. Provisions in the Convention on the Rights of the Child on equal access to education and health care reflect the principle of non-discrimination of girls and boys. Both treaties protect against violence and abuse, including gender-based violence, both of which are based on the principles of participation and non-discrimination and equal treatment. The United Nations human rights machinery is based on the Universal Declaration of Human Rights, and it is therefore important to interpret the treaty provisions in such a way that they do not undermine one another, but rather strengthen each other. The World Conference on Human Rights reaffirmed in 1993 that all human rights are indivisible and interdependent. The above illustrates the correctness of this phrase.

In interpreting the rights and obligations contained in the Convention of the Rights of the Child, all stakeholders should take into account the fact that states have obligations under the Women's Convention too, and are under an obligation to respect and advance women's human rights in all policies, thus including those aimed at promoting and protecting the rights of the child.[42] An upbringing pledge should only be considered if the different position of women and men, mothers and fathers, girls and boys, in society and in the family is sufficiently taken into account. The upbringing pledge should contribute to the elimination of existing discrimination against women. If an upbringing pledge were introduced, it should not be a measure taken in isolation, but it should be part of an all-encompassing policy aimed at improving the position of women in society and the family. Only this could render the 'double dividend'.

---

[42] Marjolein van den Brink, *Moeders in de mainstream: een genderanalyse van het werk van het VN-kinderrechtencomité*, [Mothers in the mainstream. A gender analysis of the work of the UN Children's Rights Committee.] Nijmegen: Wolf, 2006.

FROM PARENT TO GROUP PARENT
Parenthood (and Upbringing Pledge) in the Virtual Environment

Martine F. Delfos*

In this chapter the *upbringing pledge* is placed in the context of the necessity of a broad upbringing, that is in the context of the rise of a new dimension: the virtual environment (Delfos, 2006a).

What the upbringing pledge means in a broad sense is that parents promise to raise their child well and together, when a child is born. This pledge can be renewed in the case of divorce. The pledge has no substance (as of yet), and maybe it should be getting this, analogous to what is being developed in the concept of the Dutch 'parenthood plan'. The upbringing pledge is a nice concept, but the question is whether it can satisfy its expectations when it lacks a pedagogical content. It should get more substance and thereby one could think of educational support, but even more the parents themselves should be strongly aimed at it. Parents form the foundation of their child's existence. If the parents are happy with each other, it immensely enhances the chance that they will raise their children well. *Relationship* support would in many cases probably be more effective than *educational* support. It will require a pedagogical revolution to bring about such a change, but refraining from doing so would possibly be a new form of neglecting the needs of children.

1. FROM PARENT TO GROUP PARENT

We live in a society where the upbringing on the one hand is being assigned more strictly to the parents and on the other hand is freely being influenced by the 'whole' world through the panel of TV, computer and cell phones, amongst other things. We form society together, so we do have a shared pedagogical responsibil-

---

* Dr. Martine F. Delfos, Utrecht, The Netherlands, is a clinical psychologist and psychotherapist, and is specialised in working with children and adults with multiple traumatic experiences. In addition to her work as a therapist and a lecturer she has published several books and articles in the field of psychology. Email: mfdelfos@wanadoo.nl.

ity. The upbringing pledge cannot replace the societal responsibility towards education. One of the founders of pedagogy, Comenius (1592–1670), put it as follows:

> We all are citizens of the same world. To hate a human being, because he is born elsewhere, because he speaks another language, because he thinks differently about things, because he knows less or more than you do, what incomprehension! For we are all human and therefore not perfect. We all have a need for help. Nobody is without commitments towards others. (Comenius, 1667/1966).

We are at risk of losing sight of especially this last part of the words of Comenius: 'the commitments towards others'. This has to do with a changing society, in which with the industrial revolution family ties have weakened, because people moved out of the village into the city. In Africa one still can find the meaning of collective upbringing in sayings. A Nigerian saying goes: 'Ora na-azu nwa', meaning 'It takes a village to raise a child'. It expresses the necessity for a community to the growing up of the child. That this isn't a coincidence, becomes visible when we see similar sayings from other African countries:

- Lunyoro (Banyoro): *Omwana takulila nju emoi*: A child does not grow up only in one single home (Condor, De Paul, 2006).
- Kihaya (Bahaya): *Omwana taba womoi*: A child does not belong only to one parent or home (Condor, De Paul, 2006).
- Kijita (Wajita): *Omwana ni wa bhone*; en Kiswahili: *Asiyefunzwa na mamae hufunzwa na ulimwengu*: The upbringing of a child belongs to the community. (Condor, De Paul, 2006).
- Swahili: *Mkono mmoja havlei mwana*: It is not only one hand that can bring up a child (Scheven, 1981).

In our view, the expression 'It takes a village to raise a child' does not express the need for manpower in education, but the need for a great diversity to develop the potential of only one child. You need someone to give love, someone to define boundaries, someone who loves fishing, someone who knows how to handle children, someone who is strict, someone who spoils, someone who reads, someone who sports, someone who loves nature, someone who explains the working of cars to you, someone who laughs with you, someone who teases you and so on. We cannot go back to the village, but we can look for solutions that meet the need for a shared upbringing.

Perhaps the answer would be to progress from a 'parent' to a 'group parent' to share part of the upbringing with other parents – not as a pledge, not in the sense of a contract, but in a pedagogical sense, that is to decide to adhere to educational values and rules as a group of parents with a group of parents in a neighbourhood, a group of parents at school or with the parents of the peers of your child. Rules like: we do not internet from 18.00 till 20.00 in the evening. In Finland there is already a tradition that parents make these shared agreements in 'parent meetings' in primary schools. We need parents to make the upbringing pledge together, towards each other and support each other in the upbringing of their children.

The upbringing pledge seems clear, but this is no guarantee for a good upbringing. We try to raise children as well as we can, but the approach remains very often an educated guess and is prone to mistakes (Delfos, 2006a).

Japan can probably be considered the thermometer of the world. It is a thoroughly achievement oriented society, where children and adults are pushed by the highest expectations. Japanese toddlers are given lessons to prepare them for their admission exams for grammar school. Some facts from Japan show what consequences this can engender:

- 1950–1960: highest suicide figures in the world
- 1960–1980: highest figures for bullying children at primary school
- 1980–1990: highest suicide figures in young people in secondary school
- 1990–2000: hikikomori (adolescents that withdraw totally from social life and stay in their rooms at home).
- Beginning of the 21st century (2003): 850,000 drop outs who do not want to work or study.
- Beginning of the 21st century (2007): youngsters e-mail massively to the Japanese government to implore them to do something about the wave of suicide on the internet.

The last fact reminds one of the Convention on the Rights of the Child (CRC), Article 17 introduction and part e, where it is indicated that children have the right to be protected against harmful information and material. Japanese children asked the government for protection. The Netherlands is a party to the CRC; it is up to adults to protect our children and give them boundaries within which they can learn to move freely and so they can develop optimally.

2. THE VIRTUAL ENVIRONMENT

The world in which upbringing takes place in this century has changed dramatically compared to the twentieth century. The educational space up till the 21st century consisted of three environments. The *first environment* was the family. The *second environment* was the school and the *third environment* was the world outside. In the second half of the 20th century a new environment emerged, one that deserves its own status because the educational influence is vast: the media

(TV, computer, internet, computer games, video and cell phones), with the internet as the most important influence. That is why I speak of a *fourth environment*: the *virtual environment* (Delfos, 2006a).

By virtual environment I mean the fictional world that is being created by the media, where parents and children move around passively (particularly television and video) or actively and interactively (particularly the internet, computers, cell phones and gaming) – a world in which one can move around in a real way (as oneself) or in a fictuous way (with another identity and even with changing identities). The role of adolescents in the virtual environment is unmistakable. Young people make the world mobile (Lenhart et al., 2005). Adults hardly know what happens in the virtual environment; they are not very conscious of this environment, and have little understanding of it. There seems to be a generation gap between a 16 and a 20 year old (Delfos, 2006b); people above 20 hardly understand what children below 16 are experiencing. It extends even to the language, which I call virtual steno. The virtual environment is a world in its own, where you can play with millions of others online, where you form groups of virtual friends and where you have to get up at three o'clock in the night to be able to play with your friends in Japan, in order to reach a higher level together (for instance World of Warcraft = WoW). When it comes to friends in games, they want to know if it is a RLF (Real Life Friend) or an M8 (M-eight = Mate from the computer). When one of the M8's has taken a week's leave to reach a higher level, they send each other a harsh email: *Congratulations with your not having a life of your own*. It is a world where you play with a chosen identity, where nobody knows who you are and where you try to make acquintances with others carefully, a world where you interrupt your play to chat, to educate (*you have to go to bed now, it is late*) and where you support each other or cry to one's heart's content because your mother has died.

It is impossible to imagine life today without a computer. In general it is a blessing. But it has yet to be controlled. Children see a soap as *As the world turns* during breast feeding. The flexible baby brain takes in much media material, without knowing how to situate it. The baby cannot think: this is TV, I should not take this as seriously as my mother. When there is sexual content on an internet website during a night of feeding the baby, it does not think 'this is porn'. You can only consider something pornographic if you know what sex is. They have no thought frame to situate their experience. They process what they receive as information. That means that the material will become a part of their thinking frame.

Most of the time there is a second television set in the children's room. And children have use of the internet in most households, at school and at their friends' homes, and otherwise there is always the internet café.

Sex is an important subject on the internet. Children and adolescents are frequently confronted with explicit sexual material (Mitchell et al., 2003; Peter and

Valkenburg, 2006). In Mitchell's research, one quarter of the children mentioned that they were very disturbed by this material. Adolescents make clear that they find it very annoying to be continually confronted with sexual images (Delfos and Meere, in preparation). But they say that it is not possible to avoid it – you cannot enter the internet without seeing these images.

The possibilities of the virtual environment are tremendous and indispensable to modern society, but is has become some kind of uncontrollable monster of Frankenstein. What children can learn and discover through the internet is great, but the education that it brings about is not always favourable and the consequences as to the future are unpredictable.

3. EDUCATIONAL AUTHORITY

The virtual environment is an educational authority without ever being intended to be one. And in this latter lies the danger. As opposed to parents and school, the virtual environment cannot be held responsible for its actions, and in general it is little aware of its functioning as such an educational authority. Also, there is no intrinsic motivation within the internet as a whole, to keep itself consciously busy with its educational impact – first, because the internet is not a consistent whole and second because in general education and formation are not its aims. At school you can say: do not interfere, because it's my child or please intervene, because he attends class at your school. In schools you can debate about education. In the case of the internet, it is not under discussion. Of course there are a lot of informative sites on the internet that truly have education as their purpose, but even there it is not easy to separate the chaff from the wheat. Moreover, the computer is not a natural part of the life of adults, such as is the case with children, even very young children.

Media fills the blanks which have arisen from a changing world. As a parent or a couple of parents, it is too difficult to raise your children all by yourself. In daily life, television has become an important baby-sitter. The hypnotizing effect that emanates from the TV and computer is soothing. Even if the images are fast, the rate will still be lower than what a person has to process through his senses in daily life. Because of the magnitude of the media, the formation of children partly is provided by people who are not oriented towards education and who do not feel educational responsibility, but whose aim is to sell their product. In this way, commercial motives inadvertently penetrate the education of children. In advertising it is widely known that sex sells. The result is that the young child is sexualized. Ratings for television, sales figures for games and the number of hits on an internet website are in principle not based on educational values, but on commercial values. The influence on education is vast and parents very often are unaware of the impact (Greenfield, 2004) and they are taken by surprise by these effects. This influence is visible in appearances like clothing and language (w8! Virtual steno for: Wait!) but also in norms and values and in behaviour. Media often provides for idols and identification figures for no other reason than to enrich their owners.

However, the pace of development is so quick, so new and so extensive, that it is difficult to translate regular standards and values to the virtual world. *Virtual codes* have to be developed, not only since the sensible is in range through the internet, but also the non-sensical and damaging influence – not only for adults, but also for children. With one press of the button or one click of the mouse, the right of children to information and freedom of speech is respected and served, but with the same action the right of children to be protected against damaging information and damaging material is violated.

4. THE NEED TO FORM ATTACHMENTS

Rutger is 22 years old. He is very intelligent (IQ 145). He was teased and bullied when he was younger. His parents are divorced and he lives as an only child with his mother. He scarcely has any contact with his father. Rutger has been keeping himself to himself and does not leave his home anymore. Even his food is brought to his room because he even does not come out of his room to come down to eat.

Examples like these occur more and more and at an increasingly younger age. It is the same phenomenon as in Japan: hikikomori. It seems to be the case that the school dropouts are not so much children or youths that do not want to go to school, but that they are youthful people who want to be in the virtual world and are even addicted to it. The Lisbon-agreements about reducing the number of youthful people without adequate starting qualifications to find work in society will be outdated if we do not intervene in time.

Hans is 21 years old. His mother blushed at admitting that she had to steal the computer from his room because after four years of conflict, she did not have a clue anymore as how to approach him about the computer, and because he withdrew himself from all domestic contact. She placed boundaries, she talked and she gave advice. She had plenty of ideas on how to cope with the situation because she was active in assistance work, but she was no match for the appeal of World of Warcraft.

On the internet you easily make contact with many people. This is attractive, especially for people with contact and relationship problems, but it is often short-lived and superficial. People's need for longstanding relationships has not decreased, but it is getting more difficult to give it shape. The enormous increase of divorces gives expression to this fact. Life is accelerating. The consequence of this acceleration is that those emotions that are quick and fierce (anger, being in love, aggression and cheerfulness) are favoured over 'slow' emotions, such as tenderness, respect, modesty and love.

It is exactly the 'slow' emotions that attach people to one another, especially in long-term relationships. Communicating on the internet, for example chatting through MSN, meets people's need for contact. This is ideal for adolescents. While parents of previous generations noticed that their telephone bill increased dramatically during the puberty of their children, nowadays a considerable amount of the contacts of adolescents take place through the computer with the internet. The consequences of social education through communication on the internet are as yet unknown. Communication through the internet lacks a lot of non-verbal communication, especially if no image or sound is present. But smell, which unconsciously regulates people's behaviour, is absent too. The *emoticons*, the symbolic faces with emotions, cannot take over the non-verbal role. The consequence is that things are written down more strongly: the exaggeration emerges in the absence of non-verbal expression. Consequently certain things can come across incredibly harsh. Because of this, bullying on the internet has become quite a serious problem (Ybarra and Mitchell, 2004). Problems of children in the real world seem to be enhanced in the virtual world (van den Eijnden et al., 2006). Moreover children who are being bullied spend more time on the internet and additionally are even being bullied more severely (van den Eijnden et al., 2006). The internet seems to be a godsend for lonely people, but finding friends on the internet proves to disrupt their daily life (Morahan-Martin and Scumacher, 2003). Introvert children also use the internet as compensation for their lack of social skills (Valkenburg and Schouten, 2005).

There is a difference between boys and girls. Boys are more active in gaming; girls engage more in chatting, like MSN (Madell and Muncer, 2004; Meerkerk et al., 2006; Delfos and Meere, in preparation). Adolescents who have problems with their parents, use the internet more often to form online relations (Wolak et al., 2003). Depressed young people use the internet for information (Gould et al., 2002) and they have the tendency to communicate intensely with strangers and expose themselves more than young people without problems (Ybarra et al., 2005). Not only is the medium anonymous, but it is even more powerful than that: you can create an identity for yourself that fits you better. In an online game you can create a world where you are a different person. For many online games you have to pay to play, but you can also earn money with another identity. You can also deceive others with a false identity. If you do not succeed or if you are not successful enough in forming gratifying attachments in the real world, you can form relations on the internet through chatting or gaming on a fictional basis. You can have a fictional lover, you can chat with a computerized pop idol and perhaps there even is a parents.com available where you can subscribe to more pleasant – virtual – parents. The memory is probably not good enough to always distinguish real from virtual experiences.

5. VIRTUAL LIFE ENSCHEDE

In the Virtual Life Enschede research project, we are trying to find a way how to offer children and adolescents a healthy virtual development. The advantages of the computer and internet are enormous; you cannot deprive society from them anymore. But just as in the case of television, we will have to find a way to protect children. It will have to be a worldwide answer, because the internet operates worldwide – the basic digital highway is not called the www: the worldwide web, for nothing. The advertising code commission and the 'kijkwijzer' TV tool with symbols to help parents know what kind of program is being broadcasted, cannot protect against foreign TV channels. It is the same for the internet; it needs a worldwide protection code.

The results of the research in Enschede on the internet behaviour of children and young people from ten to fourteen years old (Delfos and Meere, in preparation) match the outcome of the national digital research (De Haan and 't Hof, 2007). Besides that, in the Enschede research the interviews went deeper into the subjects in order to understand the children better in relation to their internet experiences. Some of the results are:

1. Children and youngsters spend many hours a day at the computer. It is a substantial part of their life. Especially MSN and online gaming are important. Children in primary school spend somewhat less time at the computer than youngsters in the first two classes of secondary school (13–14 years old). All children who were interviewed did spend time using MSN. The time varied from 10 minutes to 5 hours a day on school days.
Three quarters of the first grades in secondary school spend more than an hour a day on MSN – girls more than boys. Boys play more computer games than girls. The computer is scarcely used for homework. If all the time that children say they spend at the computer (MSN, games, profile sites, surfing, etc.) is added up, it becomes clear that there is not much time left after school for other things. During vacations the computer use increases. Children move less, because their play behaviour is shifted to the computer room.

2. Parents rarely ask children about their experiences on the computer. For parents it is natural to ask about school or a party with friends, but they seldom ask about the – daily – experiences of children on the internet.
3. Youngsters experience a gap between the real and the virtual world. In the virtual world they dare more and they tell things more strongly. As a result, they fight more with harsh scolding and they dare tell their infatuations earlier, and they go steadily more quickly. The translation to the real world encounters many problems.
4. Many children mentioned spontaneously that they feel they are addicted to the computer, and some of them say that their parents are addicted.
5. Children and youngsters want rules, and protection. They have no problems having their parents and teachers pay attention to their internet activities; on the contrary, they ask for it. They propose reading their history – the overview of the websites they have visited recently – and their chats. They propose this as well as protection for their parents to be reassured. First graders of secondary school advised the protection of primary school children.
6. Youngsters want protection and they ask for ideas about computer use and the internet. They value it highly when adults know about computers and the internet.
7. Hardly any *virtual codes* have been developed for actions such as stealing other than the saying: it is your own fault – you should not have given your password.
8. Children see their parents as their most important guide and teachers as second in line. At the same time they point out that their parents and teachers are not always very computer-minded. Youngsters support the idea of caregivers who impose limits as a necessity, and say they miss this in their parents and teachers.
9. With regard to problems that they encounter, youngsters mentioned the seriousness, the magnitude and the fierceness of quarrels on MSN, and the sexual images they are confronted with.
10. Young people make clear that there is a kind of inflation going on through the internet with respect to serious problems (suicide, auto mutilation and anorexia), and they mention the risk of contagion of behaviour.

Children and adolescents spend much time at the computer, especially on the internet and they enjoy it enormously. Still, they experience daily the disadvantages and would like to be protected against it.

6. CONCLUSION

It is a right of children to be protected against harmful information and material (Article 17, introduction and part e of the Convention on the Rights of the Child – CRC). The CRC is in fact one vast *international educational pledge*. The time has come for countries to fulfil this pledge when it comes to the internet.

As a matter of fact, it is the adolescent from the sixties that has the world in his hands at the beginning of the 21st century: Bill Gates. Adolescents are the innovators, and they adore new gadgets. As the world becomes more and more dependent on technology, so will it be more and more dependent on adolescents. In the past century, adults still had power, but now they structurally lag behind adolescents as to knowledge of, and experience with the virtual environment. Knowledge is power and adults have a vast deficiency in knowledge in the virtual environment. But adults have the advantage of experience and life experience, and because of that they know how to place experiences into context, and assess their real value. Adolescents need adults to help them appreciate the value of their experiences.

It is up to adults to develop standards and values, virtual codes, for the virtual environment. Young people need and want to be protected in order to be free, because for real freedom you need boundaries. The upbringing pledge needs content; we have to involve the internet with respect to Article 17 part e of the CRC – as a kind of international upbringing pledge – to help children and adolescents develop in a healthy way in the virtual and the real environment.

REFERENCES

Comenius, J. A. (1667/1966). *De rerum humanarum emendatione consultatio catholica*. Pragae: Sumptibus Academiae Scientiarum Bohemoslovacae (original work from 1667).

Condor, De Paul (2006). It takes a village to raise a child. (n.d.). Retrieved April 20, 2006, from http://condor.depaul.edu/~jmcintos.

de Graaf, H., & Vanwesenbeeck, I. (2006). *Seks is een game: Gewenste en ongewenste seksuele ervaringen van jongeren op internet*. Utrecht: Rutgers Nisso Groep.

de Haan, J. & van 't Hof, C. (2007). *Jaarboek: De digitale generatie*. Amsterdam: Boom.

Delfos, M.F. (2006a). *Het maakbare kind. Opvoeding als (ver)gissing*. Amsterdam: SWP.

Delfos, M.F. (2006b). Gooi kinderen niet voor de wolven, maar stel grenzen en trotseer de protesten. *NRC Handelsblad,* September 2, 2006, p. 17.

Delfos, M.F., & Meere, W. (in voorbereiding). *Multimediagedrag van kinderen en jongeren. Praktijkgericht onderzoek naar hun beleving van multimedia en de behoefte aan interventies in het virtuele leven.*

Gould, M.S., Munfakh, J.L.H., Lubell, K., Kleinmann, M., Parker, S. (2002). Seeking Help From the Internet During Adolescence. *Journal of the American Academy of Child & Adolescent Psychiatry, 41 (10):* 1182–1189.

Greenfield, P.M. (2004). Developmental considerations for determining appropriate Internet use guidelines for children and adolescents. *Applied Developmental Psychology 25:* 751–762.

Lenhart, A., Madden, M., & Hitlin, P. (2005). *Teens and Technology: Youth are leading the transition to a fully wired and mobile nation.* Washington DC: Pew Internet & American Life Project.

Madell, D. & Muncer, S. (2004). Gender differences in the use of the Internet by English secondary school children. *Social Psychology of Education 7:* 229–251.

Meerkerk, G., van den Eijnden, R.J.J.M. & Rooij, T. van (2006). *Monitor Internet en Jongeren: Compulsief Internetgebruik onder Nederlandse Jongeren.* Rotterdam: IVO Factsheet.

Mitchell, K. J., Finkelor, D., & Wolak, J. (2003). The Exposure of Youth to Unwanted Sexual Material on the Internet: A National Survey of Risk, Impact, and Prevention. *Youth & Society, Vol. 34 No. 3:* 330–358.

Morahan-Martin, J., & Schumacher, P. (2003). Loneliness and Social Uses of the Internet. *Computers in Human Behavior 19:* 659–671.

Peter, J., & Valkenburg, P.M. (2006). Adolescents' exposure to sexually explicit material on the Internet. *Communication Research 33 (2):* 178–204.

Scheven, A. (1981). *Swahili Proverbs.* Washington DC: Universitiy of America Press.

Valkenburg, P.M., & Schouten, A.P. (2005). Developing a model of adolescent friendship formation on the Internet. *Cyberpsychology and Behavior 8 (5):* 423–430.

van den Eijnden, R., Vermulst, A., v. Rooij, T., & Meerkerk, G.J. (2006). *Monitor Internet en Jongeren: Pesten op Internet en het Psychosociale Welbevinden van Jongeren.* Rotterdam: IVO Factsheet.

Wolak, J., Mitchell, K.J., & Finkelor, D. (2003). Escaping or connecting? Characteristics of youth who form close online relationships. *Journal of Adolescence 26*:105–119.

Ybarra, M.L., & Mitchell, K.J. (2004). Youth engaging in online harassment: associations with caregiver–child relationships, Internet use, and personal characteristics. *Journal of adolescence 27:* 319–336.

Ybarra, M. L., Alexander, C., Mitchell, K.J. (2005). Depressive symptomatology, youth Internet use, and online interactions: a national survey. *Journal of Adolescent Health 36:* 9–18.

THE UPBRINGING PLEDGE AND THE FLOURISHING OF CHILDREN AND PARENTS

Doret de Ruyter[*]

1. INTRODUCTION

Parents and teachers are often targeted with pedagogical slogans, like child-centred education, competence-based learning, etc. Such slogans have a strong appeal, particularly because they seem to be grounded in the best interests of children and suggest that the pedagogical innovations will benefit children. However, they are often based on political-philosophical ideas and regularly implemented – for instance in schools – without any valid research into the pedagogical desirability and effectiveness of the proposals. Pedagogical foundations and the precise implications for children and educators are investigated only after complaints about the new practice are voiced. As an analytical philosopher of education I tend to approach all suggestions, even those that seem to be clearly positive for children and educators, critically, to analyze what a new concept precisely means and whether or not the implications of this concept are practically feasible and desirable. This I will do with regard to the notion of the upbringing pledge.

Firstly, we need to know what the concept of 'upbringing pledge' means. I aim to clarify its meaning by means of an elucidation of the concept 'promise', which is the sort of act to which a pledge belongs. Secondly, I want to investigate the implications of the aspects of the act of promising for our understanding of the upbringing pledge. This is not only a conceptual exercise, but also a normative ethical one. Thus, the first part of this chapter is not only descriptive but also evaluative in character. Thirdly, we have to investigate if the upbringing pledge is meaningful and fruitful as a practice, which in this case means a pedagogical and political practice. I focus on two questions: 1. Will institutionalizing the upbringing pledge influence the quality of upbringing? 2. Is it legitimate for a liberal democratic state to oblige all parents to make an upbringing pledge?

---

[*] Prof. Dr. Doret J. de Ruyter is Professor in Philosophy and History of Education at VU University Amsterdam, Faculty of Psychology and Education, Department of Theory and Research in Education. Her professional interests include parental responsibility and children's rights. Email: dj.de.ruyter@psy.vu.nl.

Before I begin with my critical analysis, I first want to make a positive remark about the proposal that new parents have to make an upbringing pledge. I believe it is good practice to demarcate a significant change in the life of persons with a ritual. A ritual acknowledges a new phase in a person's life, for instance that of a graduate, a spouse or member of a (religious) community. Rituals have different forms, but they tend to have most value for the person and the community within which the ritual takes place if they are accompanied by a promise of the person who is the subject of the ritual to at least maintain a fair level of quality of the practice or life phase she enters but also to aspire towards a high quality level. Examples are oaths and promises of professionals, for instance the Hippocratic Oath, a marriage vow or confirmation in the Christian churches.

2. THE CONCEPT OF 'UPBRINGING PLEDGE'

The saying "a promise is a debt" illustrates that 'promise' and 'promising' are moral concepts. By making a promise the promiser puts herself under the obligation to do what she has promised to do. In other words, a promise is not only a performative speech act that gives insight into the intention of a person; it also leads to a moral duty. Promises are a sub-class of agreements or contracts and as we know, keeping an agreement is one of the conditions of a moral community and well-ordered society. This is of course one of the reasons why Kant considered promises to be a categorical imperative. Such an imperative, unlike hypothetical imperatives, does not allow for exceptions to the duty of following it. The reason for this is not only that exceptions would lead to logical inconsistencies, but also that renouncing the unconditional character of a categorical imperative – like keeping a promise – would make cohabitation impossible in the end. For, who can one trust if a promise does not imply the duty to keep it? Thus, we attach great importance and high value to promises and the act of promising.

It is precisely the expectation that the promiser keeps her promise that is the rationale for using promises as a guarantee for the quality of practices. The question that arises is whether or not an upbringing pledge can fulfil the function of realizing a particular level of quality of upbringing. In order to be able to answer this question I will first describe the characteristics or conditions that are related to three elements of a promise or the act of promising, namely that there is a person who makes the promise: the promiser, a person to whom the promise is made: the promisee and the content of the promise. For each I aim to explicate the moral dimension of a promise and the implications for the conceptualization of the upbringing pledge and to unravel the consequences of the implementation of this pledge.

2.1. THE PERSON MAKING THE PROMISE: THE PROMISER

The promiser has to have several capacities and dispositions that are related to the act of making a promise. Someone who promises something to someone expresses an intention to act in a particular way. She commits herself to a particular action and assures to dedicate herself to realize what she has promised. To be able to do this – and here being 'able to' is used normatively, a person has to have three kinds of capacities and dispositions. Firstly, a person commits herself intentionally to a moral obligation and therefore she has to have moral dispositions (Downie, 1985; Scanlon, 1990; Watson, 2004). Secondly, she assures that she will put her will into fulfilling this intention and therefore she has to have volitional capacities (Downie, 1985). Thirdly, a person has to have insight into the actions that are expected from her as well as the situation in which she has to perform those actions. In other words, she has to have epistemic capacities (Watson, 2004). These three presuppositions regarding the promiser need further elucidation.

Firstly, we presuppose that the promiser is sincere. We expect that she has the intention to act upon her promise. Since the person who makes the promise has to understand that the other expects her to take her moral duty seriously, she has to have moral capacities and moral disposition for making such an assertion. For instance, she has to understand what the trust of others to keep her promise means, i.e. what an obligation involves and that she wants to live up to this trust. Normally we presume that promisers do have those capacities and disposition and we are therefore inclined to keep a person to the duty to fulfil what she has promised, even if it turns out that she did not take it very seriously herself. Think, for example, of an employee who makes a promise to her boss to end the pressure she is putting on her or of an acquaintance who promises to do something in return for a favour she wants that person to do for her, while both do not have the intention of keeping their promise. The first example may be called a white lie, but the second one is clearly a malicious promise. Both, however, still have the moral obligation that follows from the promise (Scanlon, 1990). The fact that they did not sincerely make the promise does not diminish their duty to fulfil what they have promised, precisely because the promisee trusted the promiser. In both cases we detest persons for not keeping their promise and we assume, although possibly in vain, that they will feel guilty about their deed. We expect their conscience to nag at them, because of their betrayal of the other's trust. Thus, promising presumes that the person has moral capacities and moral dispositions. In other words, the person who makes a promise needs to be a moral person. Such a person has the concept of duty and obligation as well as the emotions of guilt and shame.

Secondly, the promiser has to be able to influence her future acting, given that circumstances allow her to do so. In case this is diminished, we tend to relieve promisers from their promise. For example, if a friend has an unexpected accident which prevents her from keeping her promise of doing my weekly shopping, I will not blame her because she is not in a condition to do so. But equally important is that persons have the capacity to influence their will. This may normally be expected of persons. In the impressive article 'Freedom of the will and the concept of a person' (1982), the philosopher Frankfurt has in my view convincingly argued that having volitional capacities is characteristic for being a person. Persons are not only able to influence their will, but also to reflect on what it is they actually want; they have in his words 'second-order volitions'. A person is able to ask herself the question if what she wants is good for her or others and is able to change her will on the basis of the outcome of that evaluation. For instance, if I have to drive I am able to resist the temptation of drinking a third glass of wine. I do not want to fulfil this desire, because having had two glasses is already stretching the limits. I also believe it is good to have this will, because it avoids endangering others or myself. Frankfurt claims that people who do not have second-order volitions cannot be called persons; they are 'wantons'. Characteristic for this group of people is that they do not care for their will; they do not raise the question whether or not their desires are to be desired. This is only a small group of people, namely small children, addicts who do not have a compelling desire to quit their habit, severely mentally challenged people and people with severe psychiatric disorders who are completely ruled by their disorder. Such people are not able to make promises.

Thirdly, the person who makes the promise has to be able to understand what she is promising and to estimate if she is able to keep her promise. This means that she has to have insight into the conditions under which she has to keep her promise as well as in her own capacities. In other words, a promiser has to be rational and have epistemic abilities. Moreover, a promiser needs to be sensible and therefore modest in her promises, not only in their quantity but also in their content. For instance, it is wiser for most of us to promise to donate a substantial part of our income to an organization than promising to dedicate our entire life to end the famine in the third world. Of course, the epistemic capacities of a person have to be interpreted realistically psychologically, because a promise is a statement about something that needs to happen in the future and no one has a complete view of what is yet to come. If a couple has promised to yearly donate a large sum of money to Oxfam, but discover that one of their children has a rare disease and requires medication that is not covered by the insurance, they will reconsider the promise that they have made on the basis of this new information and may have good reasons to change it.

Does the proposal of the upbringing pledge meet the aspects we attribute to the person who makes a promise? If new parents make an upbringing pledge sincerely – if they have the intention to care for their children as well as they can, to raise them to their best ability and if they have a sufficient understanding of what that involves – then the upbringing pledge is valid. We may expect that the majority of adults are moral persons who are able to influence their will and understand what the upbringing pledge demands from them. Therefore, we may assume that adults are normally able to make an upbringing pledge. This observation, however, also leads to a reservation with regard to the proposal of obligating all new parents to make the pledge. If most people are moral persons, most people do not need a pledge to recognize that they need to look after their children and provide them with an adequate upbringing. They know that they have duties against their children and will fill possible knowledge or capacity gaps voluntarily. A second reservation concerns the possibility of verifying whether or not parents have the required capacities and dispositions.

With regard to the moral capacities and disposition it seems almost impossible to assess if a person will actually do what she has promised and continue to do so. This does not seem relevant, because this is precisely why persons make promises, i.e. their promise should take away such doubts because they promise to influence their will now and in the future. However, in the case of an upbringing pledge it is virtually impossible to check whether or not this pledge is made sincerely and therefore if the parent will actually do what she has promised to do.

The government can examine the volitional capacities of new parents, at least at the moment they make the pledge. It is possible to investigate whether adults are persons, particularly because specific groups of human beings are wantons who cannot influence their will.

With respect to the epistemic capacities we can argue that the government can do a lot to prepare parents for the pedagogical demands they face. Knowledge and many capacities can be taught. This could mean that the upbringing pledge has two advantages: (a) adults understand that they need many more skills and a much bigger commitment than they thought and (b) the government can be forced to offer assistance and courses in which future parents can gain knowledge and practice the required knowledge and capacities. But here the problem arises that it is almost impossible to check whether or not parents will use their knowledge and capacities in a good manner. An interesting example of a governmental public warning that went wrong is the following. Several years ago the Dutch government warned pregnant women about the consequences of smoking. The reduction in the baby's birth weight was named as one of the negative effects. For some women, however, this information was an incentive to *increase* the number of cigarettes they smoked. By doing so, they aimed at having an easy delivery.

Finally it is unclear how the government has to deal with parents who are thought to lack the required capacities and dispositions. Should the government remove the possibility to make a pledge and thereby make it impossible for them to become parents? This question and the reservations will return at various points.

2.2. THE PROMISEE

Characteristically, a promise is made to a person, who trusts the one who makes the promise that she will feel morally obligated to keep it. Additionally, a promise leads to an act that serves the interest of the person against whom the promise is made. This is certainly the case when someone asks another person to make a promise. Normally, we only ask a person to promise something if the act serves our interest and if we want to be certain that the other will do what we ask her to: "promise to be on time, because I have to go to an important meeting"; "promise not to tell anyone what I just told you, because they should not know". But also when a person makes a promise without the other asking for it, we expect the content of the promise to be beneficial to the promisee. When the mafia boss Tony Soprano in the television series *The Sopranos* says that he promises to kill the other guy if he comes into his neighbourhood again, we do not say that he made a promise but a threat (Downie, 1985).

The question of who is the recipient of the upbringing pledge seems simple: the upbringing pledge is made by parents to their children. Through their pledge parents commit themselves to guarantee that several fundamental rights of their child will be met (Van Crombrugge, 2006, p.14), for instance the right to continuous personal care and an indissoluble relationship between the child and her parents, the right to be recognized as a party with rights, and the right to proficient parents. However, the fact that the child is the subject of the upbringing pledge, does not mean that the child is the recipient of the promise. For instance, I can promise my neighbour to look after her house while she is on holiday. In this case her house is the object of my care, but obviously not the one to whom I have made my promise. In other words, are the children the object of the promise or are they the recipients?

Self-evidently, children are not able to understand the upbringing pledge when their parents first make it – Van Crombrugge suggests that the promise is renewed when a family situation changes, for instance in the case of a divorce or remarriage and of course by then children may have reached the age at which they are able to understand what parents promise – and therefore it can only be understood as an indirect promise to the child. This does not imply, however, that the child cannot be the recipient of the promise, because it is certainly possible that others act as substitute recipient for the child and keep parents to their promise if necessary. These could be civil servants, the group of professionals before whom parents made their pledge.

It is also possible to envisage the state being the recipient of the promise of parents to take good care of their child. In that case parents would promise to assist their children's development into active citizens of society which makes the child primarily the object of the pledge – although being a good citizen is normally beneficial for children too and therefore children could still be one of the promisees. Such a dimension can for instance be found in the baptism pledge that parents make to God and the church. In case of the baptism pledge there are three promisees: the child, God and the church. However, I believe it is wise to follow Van Crombrugge's intention and interpret the upbringing pledge as one that is made to the child, because children are the most important interested party of the upbringing pledge. Although members of society and the state have an interest in children being raised well and therefore could be the recipients of the pledge, children have a more profound interest in the good intentions of their parents, if only because they are completely dependent on their parents. This is the first reason why the child should be seen as the promisee of the upbringing pledge: it primarily needs to serve the interests of the child instead of those of the third parties. A second reason for suggesting that the state is not the primary recipient is that the pledge also aims to remind the state of its responsibility to educate children and not of its interests. As already mentioned, promises serve the interests – or at least alleged interests – of the promise; they do not lead to duties of the recipient. If a parent says to her child: "I promise that you have to do a lot of cleaning in the coming weeks if you walk into the house with your dirty boots again" it is not a promise but a threat like the example I gave earlier.

Finally, normally a person can be redeemed from her promise by the promisee (Downie, 1985). For example, if the neighbour whom I promised to look after her house has found a tenant during her absence, she will tell me that my care is no longer required (or less so if she does not trust the tenant completely). In that case the moral duty that followed from my promise is removed. It is also possible that the person who made the promise asks the recipient to relieve her from her obligations, because she has a new responsibility that makes it impossible for her to keep her original promise or because she discovers that she is unable to do what she promised. In both cases it should be presumed that the promisee is able to appraise her own interests in order to judge whether or not the promise does not need to be kept any longer. Of course, a third party could do this as well, but is this possible in the case of the upbringing pledge? This seems precisely what the upbringing pledge wants to prevent, although it does not preclude the possibility that circumstances may change and force parents to ask others to take over their parenting responsibilities.

2.3. THE CONTENT OF A PROMISE

A promise always concerns a future act of the promiser, which of course can also mean that the person does not do something (as in the example I gave about not telling something to others). The acts can be various, but as mentioned, it is characteristic that they are in the interest of the recipient.

The upbringing pledge is a paradigm example of 'a promise'. It clearly meets the condition that the content of the promise be in the interest of the recipient as there is hardly any doubt that unconditional love, care and upbringing are in the interest of children. I will discuss later on what the content of the upbringing pledge precisely could be, but first I need to address another issue that is related to the concept of 'promising'.

3. PROMISES AND DUTIES

Van Crombrugge proposes to make the upbringing pledge compulsory for all new parents and therefore it is important to discuss whether or not the character of a promise is undermined if all adults are obliged to make this pledge. The question is: can a compulsory speech act be called a promise? It seems to conflict with our linguistic intuition to say that a person has made a promise if she had no choice in doing otherwise. The three characteristics of a promiser have become irrelevant in the case of a promise made under pressure. But more importantly: can someone be held to the duty to keep her promise if this was imposed on her? At first sight, this does not seem to be the case, for we relieve a person of her moral responsibility if she was forced to do something. For example, we do not hold a person responsible for an immoral act if she was forced to do it at gunpoint or under another serious threat. However, there might be exceptions to this rule (Downie, 1985) and I will mention two.

Firstly, it is possible that the person who was forced to make a promise becomes intrinsically motivated to do what she was forced to promise. For example, if a bypass operation will only be paid for by an insurance company if patients promise to lead a healthy life and if non-compliance would require them to have to pay for it in hindsight, the promise is enforced. At first people will keep their promise, because they do not want to pay the bill themselves, but after a while some of them will want to keep their promise, because they realize that their changed lifestyle improves their quality of life and possibly lengthens it as well. Maybe they are even grateful to the insurance company for being forced to make the promise. Of course, this is a special case of 'promising', because it does not serve the interest of the promisee, but of the promiser herself. The change in motivation could very well be related to her own interest. However, this could also apply in case it serves the interests of those who are important to the promiser. Whether this exception is a good reason to make the upbringing pledge compulsory is a difficult question; I mention just a few complications. Obligating a person to make a promise under the expectation that the person will (come to) underwrite what she has promised is an uncertain practice as the obligation does not guarantee that the person who made the promise will act in a certain way; we cannot be certain that the person will recognize the importance of the moral obligations that follow from the promise. Moreover, such paternalistic actions of a state or public institution, particularly within a liberal democracy, have to be sparse. They can only be justified on the basis of the damage the person can do to others if the promise is not kept. I will return to this in the fourth section.

Secondly, access to certain offices is only possible if a person makes a pledge or an oath. Future Members of Parliament, military servicemen, judges or lawyers do not have a choice whether or not to make a pledge if they want to occupy such a position. But of course people have the freedom to decide if they want to become a Member of Parliament, soldier, etc. or not. Characteristic of the moral justifiability of these promise practices is that they may only be related to goods that are not necessary for the well-being of those persons themselves. In other words, the access to goods that satisfy the basic needs of people, like food, safety and shelter, may not be based on promise-making. People should be able to get these goods without having to make a promise, because they are necessary for their survival. In addition to this moral reason for rejecting such a practice, there is also a simple practical argument: the promise becomes meaningless, because people have no choice but to make the promise, whether or not they make it sincerely. The question that arises is if parenthood is a basic good. The answer to this question requires a separate article, but one remark can be made here. It is clear that parenthood is not a basic existential need. Adults can survive without being a parent. However, for most adults parenthood is a psychological basic need. It is one of the ways in which adults give form and content to the need to have relationships and empirical research has provided evidence that this is a basic psychological need (Ryan & Deci, 2001). This means that parenthood can be interpreted as a basic good, but this is not true for everyone because the basic need to have relations can be satisfied in different ways. This implies that I cannot give an unequivocal answer to the question whether making the upbringing pledge compulsory is morally justified or not. It depends on whether it is a basic need of the adults who have to make the promise.

It is important to distinguish between the obligating character of a promise and having obligations or duties. Promises generate moral obligations, but this is only meaningful if the person does not have those obligations already. Promising to do something to which one was already obligated is a meaningless promise. It would be strange, for instance, if a person were to promise to observe traffic rules or basic moral rules, like not to steal or kill senselessly. A promise has to concern acts that were not already morally or legally required when the promise was made. However, as I will state later in this article, a promise could be used to remind someone of her obligations. In that case, a person makes a quasi-promise as if she did not have the obligations already. Equally, quasi-promises can be an effective means to teach children what promising means, what duties are and which obligations people have – in other words what it means to be a moral person. However, by the time a child has developed into a moral person, her moral qualities are sufficient for her to do her duty. Moral adults want to keep their promise and therefore would believe the quasi promise to be redundant.

There could be two conclusions with regard to Van Crombrugge's proposal to oblige all parents to make an upbringing pledge. First it could be argued that obligating people to make a promise diminishes their responsibility. Although it is true that an imposed promise may reduce a person's responsibility for what she has promised – although exceptions to this apply as well, as I have mentioned – this should not be taken as the main lesson of this section. The conclusion I want to draw is that new parents do not have to be obliged to make an upbringing pledge, because they already have the duty to look after their children.

4. THE UPBRINGING PLEDGE AND QUALITY OF UPBRINGING

In order to be able to evaluate the content of the upbringing pledge and the fruitfulness of its implementation, we first have to decide which kind or level of upbringing quality the pledge aims to ensure. In order to do so it is helpful to describe two poles of those qualities, which I will call minimally acceptable upbringing and good upbringing.

In 1993 I defined minimally acceptable upbringing as the upbringing that contributes to the development of children into minimally rational, minimally moral and minimally authentic persons. Concisely put, this is a person who is able to live independently because she has the capacity to act in a way that benefits her own interest and does not harm the interests of others and to act in a way in which she would like to act and be. Good upbringing is the assistance of parents to the development of children into flourishing adults who will contribute to the flourishing of society (De Ruyter, 2007). I suggest that persons are able to flourish if they can give their own interpretation to the objective goods that are good for everyone – e.g. health, having relations, autonomy, and creative and intellectual development – and develop as optimally as possible *and* if the resulting life satisfies them. It is clear that the objective goods are general in character. This not only allows, it actually *necessitates* that persons give their own interpretation to those goods. While some will flourish in a lifelong monogamous relation, others do not want to bind themselves for too long and again another flourishes by being member of a community instead of having a single exclusive relationship.

My conception of 'flourishing' leads to four responsibilities of parents. Firstly, objective goods need to be part of their children's upbringing and their family life. In other words, parents need to introduce children into the objective goods. They also need to have found satisfying interpretations themselves. These interpretations are the ones they live by and thus share with their children. Secondly, it is important that parents inform children about the best interpretations of the objective goods and the ways in which the goods are best pursued. If children have ideas about what is an ideal way of being healthy, having relations with others, developing themselves intellectually and creatively, they are able to evaluate practices against these supreme standards and develop themselves as optimally as possible. Thirdly, parents need to assist children to become practically wise persons who are able to reflect on the interpretations of the objective goods in order to discover which interpretation will be satisfying to them. Finally, parents have to give freedom to their older children to explore which interpretation of the goods is good for them as what parents think is good for them, may not be the right interpretation of the good for their children. This means that children need to have an open future in which they can discover what contributes to their flourishing. It goes without saying that these parenting responsibilities are demanding.

Which level of quality of upbringing should the upbringing pledge aim to guarantee? Parents have a duty to offer a level of minimally acceptable education. This duty corresponds to the rights that children have against their parents. However, as I already argued, it is meaningless to ask a person to promise something to which she is already obligated. This means that it is not meaningful to ask parents to promise to offer their children minimally acceptable upbringing. This is not necessary for the role of the state either, because the state already has the duty to meet the Convention on the Rights of the Child and already has the right and duty to interfere in families when parents do not respect the rights of children. Thus, the content of the upbringing pledge needs to cover parenting acts or intentions that surpass the duties of parents. With the pledge parents would have to promise to provide good education thereby making it possible that children will be able to flourish. In itself this is not objectionable: the baptismal pledge is an example of this, but then we can make two further critical remarks. Firstly, parents usually wish the best for their children and parents who aim for the flourishing of their children already have the intention to raise their children well. Therefore, they do not have to be obligated to make an upbringing pledge to remind them of this. Secondly, the question arises whether a liberal state might ask parents to promise something that goes beyond their duty. This is a critical question, because the only sanction that seems to be available to the state is to withdraw parental authority. However, a liberal democratic state does not punish people who do not pursue a good. But what may or should the state do?

5. THE UPBRINGING PLEDGE IN A LIBERAL DEMOCRACY

In his article 'Several theses in relation to the upbringing pledge' Van Crombrugge makes the following claim: "According to the Universal Declaration of Human Rights, the upbringing pledge provides parents with the optimal possibilities to raise their children according to their own conceptions of the good life, which might be religious (2006, 16; translation by the author). I assume that he means that by making the upbringing pledge in front of a civil servant, the government is made responsible for enabling parents to fulfil their promise as making the pledge can hardly guarantee that parents will have the ability and possibility to fulfil what they have promised. By publicly promising they will provide an acceptable upbringing for their children, raising children is no longer the responsibility of parents only, but also of the state. According to Dillen this is a good thing; she argues: "by publicly explicating the promise to take responsibility, it becomes apparent that the responsibility of parents for their children is an ethical choice and not a natural process" (2006, p. 76; translation by the author). The upbringing pledge reminds parents and policy makers of the difficulties of raising children. Publicly, parents take primary responsibility for the well-being of their children and the pledge makes clear that policy makers have responsibility in assisting parents with their duty. Because parents make the pledge in front of a civil servant, everyone is publicly made aware of their respective duties.

I think it is helpful to make the public-private distinction somewhat more precise and by using the term 'political domain' as well. In my view it would be more correct to say that the upbringing pledge belongs to the political domain, which refers to the conglomerate of laws, regulations and rules that can be enforced by the government and that can be distinguished from the non-political domain. This difference can be illustrated with the distinction between a civil and church marriage. In the first case one signs up to a contract that from then on has legal consequences. In that sense, a marriage contract is political. In the case of a divorce, the parties need to meet the laws that regulate alimony, distribution of parenting responsibility, etc. The ecclesiastical marriage, on the other hand, belongs to the non-political domain. Similarly, the upbringing pledge is political, while the baptism pledge is non-political. Both pledges are made in public, but the public aspect in the first case belongs to the political domain in which the state may set the rules. The second belongs to the private or non-political domain in which the state is allowed to interfere only if basic moral rules and rights are being harmed. And while the community can have an important controlling function, its sanctions like exclusion from the community belong to the private domain.

We can also interpret Van Crombrugge's claim in another way, namely that the upbringing pledge fits into the framework of a liberal democracy. It is well-known that it is characteristic of a liberal democratic state not to have a preference for a particular conception of the good life. The government is neutral towards conceptions of the good of her citizens, unless that conception seriously harms the interests of others. The government 'only' demands of her citizens that they live their life in a way that does not infringe the freedom rights of other citizens to do the same. The government does not ask of her citizens to have a particular faith or conviction and only interferes in the lives of citizens when they violate the harm principle. Now, Van Crombrugge claims that the upbringing pledge meets the neutrality principle: the state does not ask parents to conform to a particular conception of the good life; parents are free to live according to their own convictions. I agree with him: if the content of his proposal does not oblige parents to accept a particular conception of the good life, and it does not seem the upbringing pledge has this implication, the upbringing pledge is coherent with the premises of a liberal state. However, this does not seem to be the critical issue.

The crucial question is whether or not the liberal state crosses the boundary by obligating adults to make an upbringing pledge. This depends on the way in which the upbringing pledge is supposed to function. It can be used as a strict entrance requirement by making the upbringing pledge and the concomitant expected capacities of parents a condition for parenthood. Although, the upbringing pledge does not necessarily have to be interpreted like this, Jan Willems seems to favour this version. He argues: "It should be investigated whether or not the upbringing pledge (in the future) should not be tied to the official installation of parents as educators, or even with endowing them with parenting authority" (2006, p. 97). And maybe there is something to his position: if the upbringing pledge is institutionalized, it might be wise to do it properly and make it meaningful to do so. However, there seem to be at least two problems with this interpretation. Firstly, such an interpretation necessitates that it is possible to determine that future parents have the ability and disposition to make an upbringing pledge. As I wrote in the second section, it can be investigated if adults have the necessary abilities, but it is hardly possible to ascertain if they will use them in a good manner, thus whether or not they have the expected disposition (in the long term as well). Should we deny parents about whom we have doubts their parenting responsibility? Secondly, it needs to be decided what should happen to pregnant women and their spouse or partner who do not meet these requirements. A sympathetic consequence would be that they are obliged to take a parenting course, but it becomes less friendly if it turns out they are unable to complete their course. Should these adults be denied parenthood? How certain can we be that they are unable to offer minimally acceptable education? But maybe we should read Willems' suggestion as a call to the state to recognize its duty to assist parents in meeting the criteria. In that case the government needs to ensure that it stays within the boundaries of its rights and duties to interfere in the private lives of citizens, which means that it only guarantees that the harm principle is not breached. However, if the state wants to operate within these boundaries, it is only allowed to demand from parents to keep the duties they have on the basis of their children's rights. And this is precisely Van Crombrugge's proposal. The meaning of the upbringing pledge is then that everyone who conceives a child or registers its birth at the city council, acknowledges in another way the rights of their child. However, as I have already argued, this duty is implied in parenthood and therefore does not require an additional pledge.

Equally, if a liberal democratic state wants to stay within the boundaries in situations in which parents do not meet their duties, we are forced to answer the question what is won with the upbringing pledge. Sanctions to relieve parents from their authority already exist in Dutch and Belgian law and these countries already have a measure that gives the state the possibility to interfere extensively with the way parents raise their children, namely the supervision order (OTS). Therefore, I have serious doubts about the necessity of initiating the upbringing pledge. It could be argued that parents understand why the government interferes as they made the promise to look after their child properly and raise it well. I doubt if this will be the case, but such an argument could also lead to instituting a practice in which parents who register their child are handed a paper that explains the responsibilities they have acquired. If the intention is to ensure that parents know their duties, that would suffice.

But maybe the state should not be involved at all; maybe the state should not be the party before whom parents make their pledge. In the beginning I said that an upbringing pledge might be an important ritual that signifies for adults that they are entering into a new stage of life. By making a pledge, parents are reminded that from now on they do not only live their own lives, but also have an enormous responsibility for the life of a vulnerable new person. Such a practice could be valuable. What the form and content of such a ritual would be and whether it would indeed be of value, is the subject of a different article, but it is clear that it would not have a political character. If my analysis in this chapter has been correct, a political version of the upbringing pledge is not only superfluous, but neither is there reason to suppose that it will benefit children.

6. CONCLUSION

Recently, the Netherlands was shocked by two reports, one by the University of Leiden (Van IJzendoorn et al., 2007) and one by the VU University Amsterdam (Lamers et al., 2007) about the prevalence of child abuse in our country. The VU calculated that one third of the youngsters in the Netherlands had encountered child abuse at one moment in their life and that in 20% of the cases this had taken place in the year 2005. The University of Leiden offered a lower number of prevalence, but even their number of 107,200 children being abused in 2005 is immensely shocking. The VU report showed that girls, children from minority families, young children and children raised by a single parent, have a higher risk of being abused. The report from Leiden provided evidence that a low level of education, unemployment, minority background and single parenthood are all factors that raise the risk of parents abusing their children. It seems sensible to use the knowledge of risk factors in preventing child abuse. In my view, the proposal of the upbringing pledge does not make a difference to these risk factors; none of them are diminished by an upbringing pledge.

All in all, I cannot draw a positive conclusion with regard to Van Crombrugge's proposal to oblige all new parents to make an upbringing pledge in front of representatives of the state. Both questions I raised in the beginning of this article, namely whether the upbringing pledge could provide a positive contribution to the quality of upbringing and whether a compulsory upbringing pledge would be fruitful, were answered negatively. Firstly, parents have a duty to raise their children, which results from the fact that they conceived a child. Parents who are unable to keep this duty or do not want to can already be reminded by the state that they have to do so and thus we do not need the upbringing pledge. Secondly, the Convention on the Rights of the Child already imposes on parents as well as the state a duty to guarantee that children receive a minimally acceptable upbringing and thus the upbringing pledge is not necessary for doing so. Thirdly, the state is not allowed to oblige parents to promise to pursue the flourishing of their children, because this goes beyond the boundaries of its permissible interference. Fourthly, parents who pursue the flourishing of their children, because they want the best for their children, will do so without the upbringing pledge. Thus, I believe the upbringing pledge will not have the positive consequences to the well-being of children as Van Crombrugge intended.

BIBLIOGRAPHY

de Ruyter, D.J. (1993). *Met recht ingrijpend. Een pedagogisch criterium voor het opleggen van hulp.* [*The right to intervene. A pedagogical criterion for the imposition of pedagogical help*]. Amsterdam: Buyten en Schipperheijn.

de Ruyter, D.J. (2007). *Geluk is zo gewoon nog niet* [*Happiness is not so common*]. Amsterdam: Vrije Universiteit.

Dillen, A. (2006). Als woorden meer zijn dan tekens en klanken Over de belofte en ouderschap. In: *Van huwelijkscontract naar opvoedingsbelofte* [*From marriage contract to upbringing pledge*]. Brussel: Het Hoger Instituut voor Gezinswetenschappen & Het Vlaams Centrum voor het Welzijn van Kinderen en Gezinnen.

Downie, R.S. (1985). Three Accounts of Promising, *The Philosophical Quarterly* 35, 259–271.

Frankfurt, H.G. (1982). Freedom of the Will and the Concept of a Person. In: G. Watson (Ed.), *Free Will*. Oxford: Oxford University Press (oorspronkelijk verschenen in 1971).

Lamers-Winkelman, F., N.W. Slot, B. Bijl & A.C. Vijlbrief (2007). *Scholieren over mishandeling. Resultaten van een landelijk onderzoek naar de omvang van kindermishandeling onder leerlingen van het voortgezet onderwijs* [*Students about abuse. Results of a national research into the prevalence of child abuse amongst students in secondary schools*]. Amsterdam: VUA/PI-Research (in opdracht van het WODC).

Ryan, R.M. & E.L. Deci (2001). On Happiness and Human Potentials: A Review of Research on Hedonic and Eudaimonic Well-being, *Annual Review of Psychology*, 52, 141–166.

Scanlon, T (1990). Promises and Practices, *Philosophy and Public Affairs* 19 (3), 199–226.

Searle, J.R. (1964). How to Derive 'Ought' from 'Is', *The Philosophical Review* 73 (1), 43–58.

van Crombrugge, H. (2006). Aantal stellingen in verband met de opvoedingsbelofte [Several thesis with regard to the upbringing pledge]. In: *Van huwelijkscontract naar opvoedingsbelofte* [*From marriage contract to upbringing pledge*]. Brussel: Het Hoger Instituut voor Gezinswetenschappen & Het Vlaams Centrum voor het Welzijn van Kinderen en Gezinnen.

van IJzendoorn, M.H. e.a. (2007) *Kindermishandeling in Nederland anno 2005: De nationale prevalentiestudie mishandeling van kinderen en jeugdigen (NPM-2005)* [*Child abuse in the Netherlands anno 2005: The national prevalence study into abuse of children and youngsters*]. Leiden: Casimir Publishers (in opdracht van het WODC).

Watson, G. (2004). Asserting and Promising, *Philosophical Studies, 117* (1/2), 57–77.

Willems, J. (2006). De opvoedingsbelofte van ouders in de Trias pedagogica van kinderen, ouders en staat [The upbringing pledge in the Trias pedagogica of children, parents and the state]. In: *Van huwelijkscontract naar opvoedingsbelofte [From marriage contract to upbringing pledge]*. Brussel: Het Hoger Instituut voor Gezinswetenschappen & Het Vlaams Centrum voor het Welzijn van Kinderen en Gezinnen.

THE UPBRINGING PLEDGE: A RITUAL IN SUPPORT OF PARENTS
A rejoinder to Doret de Ruyter's Critical Analysis

Hans van Crombrugge*

> "I don't accept things as they are,
> I want them the way they ought to be."
> [Christ in: E.E. Schmitt (2000),
> *The Gospel according to Pilate.*]

1. INTRODUCTION

'Will the introduction of the upbringing pledge improve the quality of upbringing?' and 'Can the government of a liberal democracy reliably and legitimately institute the practice of the upbringing pledge?' These two questions are central to Doret de Ruyter's analysis of the proposal to institute an upbringing pledge. De Ruyter concludes that such an institution is unnecessary and perhaps even undesirable.[1]

In order to debate the value of the upbringing pledge, we must first define a number of concepts. First of all, clarity is needed with respect to what exactly the upbringing pledge contains. And we must also examine what is understood by 'upbringing', 'the quality of upbringing', 'improving' the quality of the upbringing, and 'liberal democracy'. By nature, definitions of concepts are not purely descriptive, objective or neutral. Rather, they are necessarily subjective, and ever-evolving based on the conditions and beliefs of a particular time or setting. Therefore, to establish the content of these concepts, normative choices are made for which reasons should be given. These reasons may or may not be convincing, but that will always be the object of discussion. De Ruyter formulates answers to the questions raised above, based on *her* proposed definitions of concepts. If we do

---

* Dr. Hans van Crombrugge is senior researcher at the Higher Institute of Family Sciences, Brussels, (www.hig.be) where he teaches foundations of educational theory and family pedagogy. Research focuses on history of pedagogical ideas and on parenting. Email: hans.vancrombrugge@hig.be.

not share her views, and indeed are of the opinion that the upbringing pledge is a meaningful and legitimate instrument with which the government of a democratic state can improve the quality of upbringing, our disagreement is based on our differing views regarding what is at stake in the pledge. That is, what is upbringing, how should pedagogical quality and optimization be defined, and what is the role of a democratic government?

In this concluding contribution, I shall attempt to briefly indicate the points where my opinion differs from that of De Ruyter. To this end, I will examine the function of the pledge as a ritual, the assumptions implied by the pledge, the relationship between obligation and pledge, coercion and responsibility, the concept of upbringing and the resulting beliefs concerning quality and improvement of upbringing, and finally the role of the government. The thorough and exhaustive analysis of De Ruyter in fact demands an equally detailed and elaborate solution. My contribution here is an initial and limited reaction, which will be developed in detail later and elsewhere.

2. THE UPBRINGING PLEDGE AS RITUAL: THE INSTITUTION OF PARENTHOOD

The upbringing pledge is a ritual. As a ritual, the pledge reaffirms a transition. However, the ritual's function goes far beyond this acknowledgement. A ritual is a form of symbolic activity that 'cultivates' values that live in society. This 'cultivation' must be properly understood. In the pronouncement of what we find valuable, these values are confirmed and remembered in a personal way. Some will dispute the latter, since for them a ritual is precisely the opposite of authentic and genuine speech. Instead of articulating our own feelings with our own words, use is made by all of a formula that must always be used, or at least of a 'format' into which intentions are inserted. The latter, however, does not exclude the fact that it is an I (or a we) who pronounces the intentions and who reaffirms that which society expects from me (us) as parent(s). This is absolutely necessary: society in this way organizes, as it were, the processes of moral learning. This is not a quasi-pledge that one makes as if one does not yet understand its implications. On the contrary, the parents state that they know what is expected of them in raising their child and commit themselves to living up to the trust placed in them.

Yet, a ritual does not simply articulate values and ideals concerning a specific transition. The meaning and function of a ritual lies deeper than this calling to mind of ideals. In anthropology, there is a theoretical movement that emphasizes the function of rituals as instruments to provide meaning and significance to the tension that exists in society between the culture of values and the actual structure.¹ In a ritual, these ambiguities are recognized as actual but not as desirable, and it is made clear in a different way that the ideals must be realized in the face of the factuality, with individuals and society concretely pronouncing this intention. In this way, social relationships are continually established and at the same time confirmed.

In other words, as a ritual, the upbringing pledge is a symbolic transaction with a high degree of utopian and ideological content in the meaning with which Ricoeur uses these terms.² In the ritual, one affirms specific values as worthwhile and specific social relationships as actual possibilities in which these values must be given form. The ideological function of the pledge as a ritual legitimizes the existing practice, namely the assignment of the task of upbringing to parents. At the same time, there is the utopian function of the pledge that consists of putting into words the conditions of good upbringing, thereby fundamentally calling into question the link between upbringing and parenthood. The parents are installed as upbringers by the ritual of the pledge in which they pronounce their desire to raise their children in accordance with the values of the rights of the child. They recognize their child as a special person with rights to specific care. The biological relationship that appears to give them the actual right to be able to, and to be required to, raise 'their' child, is thus confirmed and at the same time radically called into question: it is imposed as a relationship that is only legitimate on the condition that they respect the child as a developing, learning person through care and upbringing.

Whether or not the parents have the intention to be unconditionally present for their child and whether or not they know their obligations as upbringers, is not of essential importance to the meaningfulness of the pledge as a ritual. In what follows, we will examine whether the meaningfulness of the pledge as a pledge is in fact important. This consideration is not relevant to the meaningfulness of the pledge as a ritual. Here it concerns the societal institution of the task of bringing up children incumbent on the parents, which is realized in and through the pronouncement of the upbringing pledge. It already follows from the establishment of the pledge as a ritual that the meaning of the pledge should not be sought in improving the quality of upbringing, if this is understood as preventing specific problems or realizing specific behavioural outcomes in the child. In our introductory article mention was made of the cultural meaning (as contrasted with the instrumental-technical), i.e. the symbolic (ideological and utopian-functional) connotation of the ritual.

---

1   We are inspired here by: V. Turner (1969), *The ritual process: structure and anti-structure*. Ithaca N.Y.: Cornell University Press; C. Bell (1997) *Ritual. Perspectives and dimensions*. Oxford: Oxford University Press, p. 40 ff.; as well as: V. Neckebrouck (2005) 'Kerkgangers, berejagers en maskers. Ritueel en hypochrisie', in: P. Cortois & V. Neckebrouck (ed.), *Maskers, missen en meesters. Ritvelen in en uit de marge*. Kapellen-Kampen: Peckmans – Klement, pp. 21–70.
2   P. Ricoeur (1997), *L'idéologie et l'utopie: deux expressions de l'imaginaire social*. Paris: Seuil.

3. THE UPBRINGING PLEDGE AND ITS ASSUMPTIONS: OBLIGATIONS VERSUS FACTS

According to De Ruyter, those who pronounce a pledge must possess a number of abilities and dispositions. It must be assumed that the persons making a pledge are sincere. They should be moral persons in possession of the concepts of duty and obligation as well as the emotions of guilt and shame. In the second place, these people must be able to influence and determine behaviour. Thirdly, those who pledge something must be able to understand what it is they are promising and be able to assess whether the promise can be met. Therefore, parents who pronounce an upbringing pledge should have the intention to care for and raise their child in the best possible way and they must be able to appreciate what all of this implies.

De Ruyter draws two conclusions from this starting point. Either parents have these moral dispositions and volitional and epistemological skills, in which case they do not need the pledge to realize this, or, parents fall short in one of these areas. Who, however, is in a position to know that with certainty? Who can say whether people are sincere or not? Who can know whether they will properly use this knowledge? And what then will happen with these parents and the parent-child relationship?

Our point of departure is that the responsibility of the parents as upbringers is so vast that everything must be done to make them aware of this and to support them. An institution such as the pledge serves this purpose. Not only is it a support in itself, it can indeed also be seen as a moment in a process of growth that can be expected of parents.

This educational and learning process, however, must be properly understood. It is not so much a question of transferring knowledge and exercising skills, with a test being required at a certain moment to see whether one is properly equipped to make the upbringing pledge. As experience in the case of preparing, selecting and educating foster parents shows, the preparatory formation must be understood as a process of becoming aware and a form of self-selection. Candidate foster parents are made aware of all that foster parenthood implies. Not only is knowledge passed on, but group discussions are held in which the experts are not only social workers but also experienced foster parents. During such a process of formation, a reflection process is initiated in the candidate that clarifies the learning opportunities of the candidate. The thought process in the parents is initiated through the confrontation of one's own intentions and expectations with the demands and expectations of the reality of foster parenthood. A view is provided of the suitability of the candidate-parent; it becomes clear during the preparation whether the candidate is willing and able to learn, to grow in the task of bringing up children, to deal constructively with problems, to search for assistance and support – and to accept it – when needed. This experience teaches us that the candidates attain a high level of self-selection and that in this way foster parents are well prepared.[3] In other words, the objection that one has or can have no idea in advance concerning the presence of what might be expected from parents in order for them to responsibly assume the task of bringing up children, can be refuted based on experiences with the existing practices of preparing foster parents.

Of course, one can never know whether parents are sincere and how they will act in the future. The associated objection that an upbringing pledge can change nothing of this also remains. Indeed, the freedom of people and the complexity of the upbringing mean that this is essentially unpredictable. This unpredictability is not overcome by the pledge, nor denied. On the contrary, the unpredictability of people and relationships is precisely an argument for introducing the pledge in order to deal constructively with this unpredictability. We can never know what the future will bring, how we ourselves will evolve, what will happen with the children, what the world will look like, etc. We cannot see today what responsible parenthood concretely will consist of tomorrow and the day after. Everything is possible, but not everything is desirable. Not everything is controllable, but much can be prevented. We have to dare to take risks, but we may not be reckless and unprepared with respect to the upbringing. The least we should and can do is to cultivate a fundamental attitude of pedagogical level-headedness. The pledge is both an expression of and a support to this attitude. 'Whatever happens, we parents will be there for you.' As good parents, we know that much can and will happen, and we have prepared ourselves as best we could. The children may and should be certain of one thing: even if we as parents don't (yet) know it all, we will do our best. And to 'doing our best' belongs the best possible preparation and the readiness to allow ourselves to be helped and supported. All of this is in the 'interest of the child': an 'interest' that we ourselves may not arbitrarily fill, but the core elements of which are established as the rights of the child.

From this perspective, the question is not so much who may pronounce the pledge or how to establish whether parents can provide the requisite guarantees. By introducing the pledge, we give the parents the chance in the first place to reflect on the question of whether they really want to raise children. This institution also sends out the signal that the task of bringing up children presupposes a number of dispositions and possibilities that, however, in the first place are not something that must be established objectively, but that parents personally must realize and cultivate in freedom.

---

[3]   For nuanced visions on educating parents, see: L. Vandemeulebroecke, H. Van Crombrugge, J. Janssens & H. Colpin (ed.) (2006; 2002), *Gezinspedagogiek. Deel II: Opvoedingsondersteuning.* Antwerp: Garant (and concerning foster parenthood in particular, the articles by Meulenbergs and Robbroeckx).

The point of departure of the institution of the pledge is not that not everyone is suitable to be a parent (even if that is the case). The point of departure is that children have a right to and a need for good upbringers and these ideally are the parents, and thus that the parents should properly understand what they are getting into so that they can seek the support they need, and also that parents must be supported in every way possible by the extended community. By offering parents the possibility of pronouncing the upbringing pledge, government and society give parents the signal that they must – but also can – be good parents. The institution of the pledge is a sign of great trust in the possibilities of the parents. By instituting the pledge for all parents, we are assuming that all parents are capable in principle of being upbringers. Giving parents the chance to pronounce the pledge is evidence of great trust in the possibilities and the sincerity of parents. To put it more pointedly – and somewhat paradoxically – that which should be expected to be present in parents in order to pronounce the pledge, namely sincere and good intentions, is precisely pronounced in the institution of the pledge and in this way actively adopted. This can and often will be a counterfactual assumption, but at the same time is an unavoidably necessary assumption. To use an analogy: to know whether it is worthwhile to enter into a discussion with someone, we must presume that this person has something to say. However, we will only know whether this person has something to say in the discussion itself, and that is why we should enter into discussion with this person assuming that he or she has something to say. By entering into discussion with someone, we as it were, force this supposition on this person. Whether he wants to say something or actually will say something is unknown and out of our control (because this after all would no longer be a discussion). By entering into discussion, however, we are treating the other as a discussion partner, as someone who has something to say. By analogy, we appoint parents as upbringers by making it possible for them to pronounce the upbringing pledge. They are not required to pronounce the pledge, but then they may not assume the task of bringing up children. If they wish to be an upbringer, they not only must pronounce the pledge, they must also want to pronounce it and thus commit themselves through that which we as a community ask to be promised on behalf of the child. We cannot and do not wish to know whether or not someone is sincere. Taking someone seriously as a person, however, means to assume that he is sincere. It follows from this that he can be called to account and that he cannot say that he did not mean or did not know what he said. To the latter applies the truism: 'a promise is a promise'.

Because of this latter unavoidable aspect of the pledge, we must ensure as much as possible that those who make a pledge are aware of what they promise and of that to which they are committing themselves. Thus, people must be prepared so that they are capable of pronouncing the upbringing pledge in a well thought out way. As such, conditions can indeed be attached to those who wish to make the pledge. It can reasonably be expected that everyone is prepared in the best possible way for a difficult task with great responsibility, and the government can and must also be able to demand this as a prerequisite for making the upbringing pledge.

4. THE UPBRINGING PLEDGE AND ITS STAKEHOLDERS: EVERYONE IS COMMITTED TOGETHER

The fact that the upbringing pledge is pronounced by parents who wish to be the upbringers of their child is clear.[4] But to whom must these people direct themselves? To the child? To the government? To society?

The upbringing pledge is directed at various interested parties. The first is of course the child. It is the child who needs a sustainable, caring and guiding relationship with his parents, and on the basis of this is entitled to parents who are committed to unconditional care and the best possible upbringing. Because the child is incapable of hearing the pledge – at least in the case of newborn babies – it is recommended that the child be represented by an adult. This person represents the child. We can think here of a sort of godfather or godmother, where someone (from the family or from the primary network of the parents) personally acts as a representative of the child.[5] In pronouncing the pledge, the parents direct themselves to the person representing the child. In addition to the godfather/godmother, there is also a representative from the government who guarantees the care and the upbringing of each child and who through the pledge is addressed by the upbringers in his responsibility to assist them in all possible ways. In addition to the godfather/godmother and the representative of the government, it is also meaningful to include witnesses. They represent every citizen in society who in principle is responsible for the well-being and growth of each child in society, regardless of relationship, or geographical or psychological proximity to the child.

We until now have neglected one of the parties with the greatest stake: the other parent. In the standard situation, the two parents each pronounce the pledge personally and in this, they also and especially direct themselves to the other parent. The promise to the child 'we will be there for you' – also has as intent that,

---

[4] In the following, I assume the 'simple' situation of two parents with a common child. We can later reflect on other situations in which the relationship and life situation are more complex.

[5] Thus, this is not the same as a godfather/godmother in the Catholic Church who does not represent the child at his/her Baptism, but in fact represents the church and has the task of supervising the proper education in the faith (cf. *Kathechismus van de Katholieke Kerk (version 1997)*, art 1255, source: www.rkdocumenten.nl).

whatever might happen between the parents, the 'we' that is established in the common care for the shared child is in principle indissoluble. Even if the couple parts ways and the partners enter into new relationships, together they still remain the parents of the child. Joint contact, care and upbringing will be pursued out of interest for the child.[6]

We will return later to the question of what one precisely pledges to the child, the other parent, society and the government. First, we would like to say something about the meaning of an imposed pledge and the relationship between pledge and obligation.

5. THE PLEDGE AND ITS BINDING CHARACTER: THE DEMAND OF THE CHILD AS A MORAL CLAIM

By making a pledge, one imposes obligations on oneself. An imposed pledge requires one to take obligations upon oneself. Is this justifiable? Can people be held responsible for something they are obliged to do?

Let's approach this problem from a different angle and use as our point of departure the child's need for and right to a sustainable relationship with the parents who will care for and raise him or her. In other words, a demanding need arises from the perspective of the child for people willing to assume and maintain an enormous degree of commitment. The mere fact of the child's existence places a great responsibility on the parents and in fact on all adults. By virtue of this birth and dependent state, the child demands much of his parents. This demand on the part of the child can be addressed in various ways: one can dedicate oneself to the child, one can leave it to others. But whatever one does: it is an answer to the demand of the child, an answer that may or may not do justice to the child. Thus fundamentally it is not society or the government that forces one to make a pledge: it is the child itself that places the obligation to provide an answer to his demand for justice.[7]

---

[6] We are not able to develop this further here, but there is sufficient evidence in support of the fact that divorce endangers the interests of children, and that children not only need as little conflict as possible between the parents, but also and especially need a relationship with both parents. Cf. H. Van Crombrugge (2007), 'Werelden overbruggen. Kinderen en scheiding', *Rondom gezin*, 28(1): 2–17.

[7] In this sense, Jonas can indeed state that responsibility for the child is one of the fundamental models of responsibility, see: H. Jonas (1984). *Das Prinzip Verantwortung. Versuch einer Ethik für die technologische Zivilisation*. Frankfurt: Suhrkamp, p. 184 ff.; pp 234–244. Cf. also H. Van Crombrugge & M. Heylen (1999), 'Een ethisch-relationeel perspectief op de ouder-kindrelatie', in: L.Vandemeulebroecke, H. Van Crombrugge & J. Gerris (red.), *Gezinspedagogiek Part I: Actuele thema's in onderzoek en praktijk*, Antwerp: Garant, pp.65–86; R. Burggraeve (2007), 'Ouderlijke verantwoordelijkheid voor kinderen. Antropologische en ethische krachtlijnen

One is required to answer in word and deed. In instituting the upbringing pledge, the government creates a form in which to pronounce that answer publicly. The government that imposes the pledge, is acting here on behalf of the child who himself is unable to ensure his rights. The argument that an obligation on the part of the parents imposed by the government would make the parents less responsible for what happens to their child, also lacks credibility. An analogy: in Belgium, citizens are obliged to vote; does this make them less responsible for the election result? I don't think so.[8]

The judgement of De Ruyter that promising to do something that is compulsory or expected is an empty promise, is then also unfounded. In addition to the above-mentioned arguments, we could also present the arguments that follow from the functions of the pledge as a ritual. It is indeed meaningful to require people to explicitly and formally think and recall something that they already know and desire, because this is the way values are learned and cultivated.[9]

De Ruyter introduces still another consideration in her argument: one cannot impose conditions on people for access to something to which they have a right. De Ruyter contends that having and relating to children is a basic need, so one cannot deny this to someone. I can accept that people have a basic need for human relationships. I can also accept that people have an existential need for a relationship with their own children. The theory and the experiences of Boszormenyi-Nagy concerning the 'invisible loyalties' in the parent-child relationship, are very convincing on this point.[10] One cannot accept, however, that a right to enter into such relationships simply follows from this need. The child is not an object to satisfy a need, just as the relationship with the child cannot be an instrument to satisfy parental needs. As a person, the child has the right to relationships that do justice to him as an individual person. The rights of the child are regulative principles to give form to relationships that do justice to the child as a developing, learning person. Conditions indeed may and should be imposed on parents concerning the way they wish to pursue the relationship with their children and it indeed can be demanded of them that they formally promise to realize these principles of the rights of the child in word and deed in the parent-child relationship.

This brings us to that what the upbringing pledge is all about: the quality of the upbringing in light of the rights of the child.

---

vanuit Emmanuel Levinas', in: *Beseffen alle ouders wat verantwoordelijk-zijn voor een kind is?* Brussels: Hoger Instituut voor Gezinswetenschappen, pp. 37–56.

[8] The analogy also applies in that compulsory voting is not an obligation imposed by the government, but rather a form that the government makes available in order to do justice to one's duties as a citizen, to what oneself is required to do as a reasonable human being, namely to participate in the building of society.

[9] The functioning of the pledge can thus be compared to '*memorials*': reminders of what we already know or are expected to know. What else could be the meaning of commemorating the end of the First and Second World War or the horrors of the concentration camps?.

[10] See Van Crombrugge & Heylen (1999) in footnote 7.

6. THE PLEDGE IMPROVES THE QUALITY OF UPBRINGING: IT CONFIRMS AND ESTABLISHES RESPECT FOR THE RIGHTS OF THE CHILD

Finally, according to De Ruyter, the meaning of the upbringing pledge must be measured against its optimizing effect on the upbringing. Is the upbringing improved because of it? Does a pledge increase the quality of the upbringing? What, however, is 'quality' upbringing?

In the proposal for the upbringing pledge, I use a different view of upbringing than De Ruyter and thus also of the quality of upbringing.[11]

The difference between a minimally acceptable upbringing and good upbringing is a difference in function of the objectives intended in and through the relationship. The limited objective is raising children into minimally rational, minimally moral and minimally authentic persons. The ambitions of a good upbringing extend further: the development of children into flourishing adults who will contribute to the flourishing of society. To achieve these objectives, parents need to bring up their children. Upbringing is of a minimally acceptable quality if that which is necessary to reach the minimum objective is present; if that which is necessary to achieve the objective of flourishing is present, one can speak of a good upbringing.

This is an interesting and in many ways fruitful approach, but it is not the one I use to describe the pedagogical significance of the upbringing pledge. Instead of an instrumental definition of quality, I work with a relational definition.[12] This difference between an instrumental and relational approach could already be felt in the question of whether or not responsibility would diminish due to the obligatory character of the pledge.

What do I mean by the instrumental determination of quality of upbringing? According to the instrumental or technical view of upbringing, a responsible upbringer is a person who knows which objectives he should pursue in the upbringing of a child and who has the requisite dispositions, capabilities and skills to achieve these objectives. Ideally he knows what the effects of his pedagogical activities will be, which objectives are desirable and how realizable these are. If he were not to pursue these, he would be irresponsible.

I understand upbringing more as a relationship between people who in principle are equal (despite all the differences between them). Like all relationships, parent-child relationships are unpredictable in principle. Making relationships predictable is only possible by allowing no room for that which is foreign, the

---

[11] To this for that matter also belongs a different interpretation of the notion of responsibility.
[12] Cf. H. Van Crombrugge (2007), 'Goede bedoelingen volstaan niet altijd', in: *Beseffen alle ouders wat verantwoordelijk-zijn voor een kind is?* Brussels: Hoger Instituut voor Gezinswetenschappen, pp. 83–88.

individual and the unknown of the subjectivity of the persons involved. Responsibility can then in no way be understood as knowing what will and should happen and responsible actions are then not predictable actions. Responsibility begins with recognizing the unpredictability of the relational event. Responsible activity is then creating and maintaining the space for the unpredictability of the coming together of strangers and unknown persons. A relationship, however, only has a real future to the extent that the other can show himself as another. Responsible activity is not desiring to establish the future of the child in goals to be achieved, but quite the contrary, giving the future the chance to remain truly open.

In the latter view, the quality of upbringing is defined in relational terms: the manner in which one deals with the child is decisive (whatever the effects will be in the end). This is not to say that the upbringer has no objectives, but rather that neither the nature of the objectives, nor the effectiveness of the upbringing activities are determinative of the quality of the upbringing. The quality of the relationship is measured in relational values. These values are derived from that to which a person in a relationship is entitled as a person and from that which makes a relationship a dignified one.[13] The rights of the child are for me a formulation of that to which the child is entitled as a person. The rights of the child cannot be understood as the minimum requirements of their upbringing. They are the regulative principles to which each upbringer should strive if he intends to act responsibly, i.e. he wants the relationship with the child to be rooted in human dignity. That is why these rights must be affirmed in the upbringing pledge. If the parents wish the relationship with their child to be recognized, affirmed and supported as a responsible relationship, it follows that they must commit themselves to the realization of a specific quality of the relationship: the dignity of the parent-child relationship.[14]

In the upbringing pledge, children's rights are affirmed and cultivated as human rights. I have elsewhere stated that the change from parent to upbringer occurs in the recognition on the part of the parents of the child as this particular person. Parents should not see in the child purely their 'own' child, not a purely

---

[13] If one then still desires to measure the effectiveness of actions – is the upbringing improved because of it? This efficacy should not be defined in terms of the behaviour of the child, but in the first place in terms of the relational quality of the parental behaviour.

[14] In the light of this distinction, the question can be asked whether the rights of the child could not be the basis of a more fundamental critique of De Ruyter's criterion than those that were expressed with respect to her dissertation; for this critique, see: J.C.M. Willems (1998), *Wie zal de opvoeders opvoeden? Kindermishandeling en het recht van het kind op persoonswording*, Maastricht (diss.), p. 362 ff. The abstract nature of the criterion proposed by De Ruyter after all does not refer so much to the fact that social workers do not work with the concepts of rationality, authenticity and morality, but rather chiefly to the fact that social workers do not employ instrumental but rather relational criteria (to be sure often in the delusion that these are instrumental).

developing being, not a purely learning being. The pedagogical outlook sees in the child the developing, learning 'other and foreign' person and wishes to take him seriously in his capacity as a special person.[15] The upbringing pledge can then be understood as a ritual in which this 'change' – this recognition and affirmation – is given a symbolic aspect. The upbringing pledge expresses the quality of the parent-child relationship as an intrapersonal relationship. In other words: there is a paradoxical nature to parenting. A sense of responsibility and intimacy comes from the sense of possession – this is my child. Yet at the same time, one needs to grasp this separate 'otherness' to embody the quality of dignity and freedom. It is not easy for many parents to integrate this emotional attachment and this mental detachment. The upbringing pledge is an opportunity to introduce this outlook on parenting and impart almost a sense of 'nobility' of the 'parenting path'.

Within this framework, parents can and must raise children in accordance with their philosophical and religious convictions, according to their conceptions of the good life and a good upbringing, which brings us to our final theme: liberal democracy and parenthood.

7. THE UPBRINGING PLEDGE IN A LIBERAL DEMOCRACY: THE UPBRINGING OBLIGATION IMPOSED BY THE GOVERNMENT

Can a government in a liberal democracy demand an upbringing pledge of parents? I am not an expert in political philosophy, but I see no tension between embracing the proposal for an upbringing pledge and that of a democratic order.

First of all, a democratic state that wishes to be as neutral as possible with respect to divergent conceptions of the good life, also needs civil rituals and its own symbols. Banning rituals in communities of faith appears to me neither recommended nor possible. The position of the government not only cannot be filled neutrally, but should also be one of transcending and holding together individual communities.[16] As citizens, people must be able to live together in society and not only as members of the communities that together make up society.

The upbringing pledge is a civil ritual and is of a different order than for example a church Baptism. In the 19th century nation states, an upbringing pledge would probably have comprised national citizenship: the parents should commit themselves to raising their children into national citizens and in so doing con-

---

[15] H. Van Crombrugge (2004/1999), 'Mijn kind is een vreemde. Ik ben een vreemde voor mezelf. Verwantschap, belofte en vergiffenis,', in: H. Van Crombrugge, *Verwantschap en verschil. Over de plaats van het gezin en de betekenis van het ouderschap in de moderne pedagogiek.* Antwerp: Garant, pp. 167–177.

[16] And also of supporting these communities.

sider themselves representatives of the nation state.[17] Present-day states have committed themselves through multiple treaties to honouring human rights. An example of this is the Convention on the Rights of the Child. By ratifying such a convention, states commit themselves to realizing its values and ideals.

This, however, does not yet involve the commitment of individual citizens. In instituting the upbringing pledge, in which parents (should) commit themselves to a dignified relationship with their children in accordance with the values and ideals of the rights of the child, the government is also creating an instrument that realizes values and ideals in families. Thus, not only is such an instrument not superfluous as De Ruyter states, but it is truly a necessity with which the government by no means exceeds its authority. The liberal democratic state after all is not simply neutral, but rather it stands for values and ideals that are translated into agreements in different domains. Each government, in the light of its authority, has the obligation to translate these values and ideals into its areas and forms of authority and to devise instruments that realize these values in practice.

Liberal democratic governments should also support parents instrumentally and culturally to be good parents – also institutionally – for example via the upbringing pledge. After all, who else will bring up the parents?

---

[17] Fichte can then be considered an example of someone who was unable to believe in this possibility, and thus proposed removing children from parents at birth and raising them in state institutions as German citizens who later in turn would be able to raise their children themselves.

MAASTRICHT SERIES IN HUMAN RIGHTS

The *Maastricht Centre for Human Rights* supervises research in the field of human rights conducted at Maastricht University's Faculty of Law. This research is interdisciplinary, with a particular focus on public international law, criminal law and social sciences. The titles in the Series contribute to a better understanding of different aspects of human rights *sensu lato*.

Published titles within the Series:

1. Ineke Boerefijn, Fons Coomans, Jenny Goldschmidt, Rikki Holtmaat and Ria Wolleswinkel (eds.), *Temporary Special Measures. Accelerating de facto Equality of Women under Article 4(1) UN Convention on the Elimination of All Forms of Discrimination against Women* (2003)
ISBN 90-5095-359-X
2. Fons Coomans and Menno T. Kamminga (eds.), *Extraterritorial Application of Human Rights Treaties* (2004)
ISBN 90-5095-394-8
3. Koen De Feyter and Felipe Gómez Isa (eds.), *Privatisation and Human Rights in the Age of Globalisation* (2005)
ISBN 90-5095-422-7
4. Ingrid Westendorp and Ria Wolleswinkel (eds.), *Violence in the domestic sphere* (2005)
ISBN 90-5095-526-6
5. Fons Coomans (ed.), *Justiciability of Economic and Social Rights* (2006)
ISBN 978-90-5095-582-9
6. Jan C.M. Willems (ed.), *Developmental and Autonomy Rights of Children: Empowering Children, Caregivers and Communities. 2nd revised edition* (2007)
ISBN 978-90-5095-726-7
7. Alette Smeulers and Roelof Haveman (eds.), *Supranational Criminology: Towards a Criminology of International Crimes* (2008)
ISBN 978-90-5095-791-5
8. Hans van Crombrugge, Wouter Vandenhole and Jan C.M. Willems (eds.), *Shared Pedagogical Responsibility* (2008)
ISBN 978-90-5095-813-4

www.ingramcontent.com/pod-product-compliance
Ingram Content Group UK Ltd.
Pitfield, Milton Keynes, MK11 3LW, UK
UKHW060949220426
5322IPUK00034B/634